THE CHRISTIAN

By the same author:

SALVATION, THE BIBLE, AND ROMAN CATHOLICISM

THE CHRISTIAN

Following Christ as Lord

WILLIAM WEBSTER

THE BANNER OF TRUTH TRUST

THE BANNER OF TRUTH TRUST
3 Murrayfield Road, Edinburgh EH12 6EL
PO Box 621, Carlisle, Pennsylvania 17013, USA

★

© *William Webster 1990*
First Published 1990
ISBN 0 85151 577 0

★

Scripture quotations are taken from the
New American Standard Bible, © *1960, 1962, 1963,*
1968, 1971, 1973, 1975, 1977 by The Lockman
Foundation. Used by permission.
Quotations taken from the books, *The Gospel According to Jesus* by John
MacArthur, Jr. Copyright © 1988 by John F. MacArthur Jr., and *In
His Image* by Dr. Paul Brand and Philip Yancey. Copyright © 1984,
1987 by Dr. Paul Brand and Philip Yancey, are used by permission of
Zondervan Publishing House.
Typeset in 10½/12pt Linotron Plantin
At The Spartan Press Ltd, Lymington, Hants
Printed and bound in Great Britain by
BPCC Hazell Books
Aylesbury, Bucks, England
Member of BPCC Ltd.

Contents

1: *The Indwelling Spirit*

In Romans 8:1–17 Paul expounds the wonderful truth of the indwelling of the Holy Spirit in the life of every Christian. This is *the* major evidence that an individual is truly a Christian, for Romans 8:9 states that if a person does not have the Holy Spirit dwelling in him he is not a child of God: 'However, you are not in the flesh but in the Spirit, if indeed the Spirit of God dwells in you. But if anyone does not have the Spirit of Christ, he does not belong to Him.' Jesus, in his conversation with Nicodemus, emphasizes that Christianity is a matter of receiving a new life, of being 'born again' by the Spirit of God: 'Truly, truly, I say to you, unless one is born again, he cannot see the kingdom of God . . . That which is born of the flesh is flesh, and that which is born of the Spirit is spirit. Do not marvel that I said to you, "You must be born again"' (*Jn. 3:3, 6–7*). It is the Holy Spirit who regenerates the heart and communicates new life to a sinner, causing him to be born a second time.

As Romans chapter 8 goes on to emphasize, the Holy Spirit is not only the source of new life, he is also the sphere in which the Christian life is lived. The Christian life is a spiritual, supernatural life. Note the contrast given in Romans 8:3–9:

> For what the Law could not do, weak as it was through the flesh, God did: sending His own Son in the likeness of sinful flesh and as an offering for sin, He condemned sin in the flesh, in order that the requirement of the Law might be fulfilled in us, who do not walk according to the flesh, but according to the Spirit. For those who are according to

the flesh set their minds on the things of the flesh, but those who are according to the Spirit, the things of the Spirit.

These verses set forth a contrast between two kinds of people. Those who walk according to the flesh and those who walk according to the Spirit. There are those who are in the flesh, who set their minds on the things of the flesh, who are disobedient to the law of God and who cannot please God. In contrast there are those who are in the Spirit, who set their minds on the things of the Spirit, and who walk in obedience to the Word of God. This is obviously a contrast between a true Christian and an unbeliever. It is *not* a contrast between a carnal Christian and a spiritual Christian for Romans 8:9 specifically makes a distinction between being 'in the flesh' and being 'in the Spirit', and emphasizes that what distinguishes between the two is the indwelling of the Holy Spirit. In other words, those who are in the flesh are not indwelt by the Holy Spirit and are therefore not true believers: 'However, you are not in the flesh but in the Spirit, if indeed the Spirit of God dwells in you.'

This contrast tells us something of vital importance. It shows that the Christian life is lived in and by the Spirit and manifests itself in specific and identifiable ways. The life of a Christian is one that has been reoriented from 'the things of the flesh' to 'the things of the Spirit'. It is a life that has been transformed: the expressions 'born again' and 'new life' mean no less. A radical change takes place in every person who is regenerated by the Holy Spirit: 'If any man is in Christ, he is a new creature; the old things passed away; behold, new things have come' (*2 Cor. 5:17*).

If indeed life in Christ is a matter of becoming a new creation significant changes in the moral character of an individual will follow inevitably. The whole life, from the inside out, will be transformed. Romans 8:16 describes the Holy Spirit witnessing with our spirit that we are the children of God. One of the ways that he does so is by bearing witness to the changes that have been effected in our lives by his supernatural power. Jonathan Edwards comments on the nature of this witness of the Holy Spirit:

> The manner in which the word *witness*, or *testimony*, is often used in the New Testament, viz. holding forth evidence from whence a thing may be argued and proved to be true. Thus, Heb. ii. 4. God is said to *bear witness, with signs and wonders, and divers miracles, and gifts of the Holy Ghost.* Now these miracles are called God's witness, not because they are of the nature of *assertions*, but *evidences* and proofs. So . . . John v. 36. 'But I have a greater witness than that of John; for the works which the Father hath given me to finish, the same works that I do, bear witness of me, that the Father hath sent me.' . . . And when the Scripture speaks of the *seal* of the Spirit, it is an expression which properly denotes – not an immediate voice or suggestion, but – some work or effect of the Spirit left as a divine mark upon the soul, to be an evidence, by which God's children might be known . . . The *seal of the Spirit* is called the *earnest of the Spirit*, in the Scripture. 2 Cor. i. 22. 'Who hath also sealed us, and given the earnest of the Spirit in our hearts.' And Eph. i. 13, 14. 'In whom, after that ye believed, ye were sealed with that holy Spirit of promise, which is the earnest of our inheritance, until the redemption of the purchased possession, unto the praise of his glory.' . . . The inheritance that Christ has purchased for the elect, is the Spirit of God; not in any extraordinary gifts, but in his vital indwelling in the heart, exerting and communicating himself there, in his own proper, holy, or divine nature . . . Therefore this *earnest* of the Spirit, and *first-fruits*, which has been shown to be the same with the *seal* of the Spirit, is his vital, gracious, sanctifying influence, and not any immediate suggestion or revelation of facts.[1]

[1]Jonathan Edwards, *A Treatise concerning Religious Affections*, in *The Works of Jonathan Edwards*, Volume I, (Edinburgh: The Banner of Truth Trust, reprinted 1974), pp. 273–274.

Edwards is saying that the witness of the Holy Spirit that we are children of God is directly related to his indwelling and to the evidence of his presence by means of a sanctified life. If a person has become a true Christian, he is one who has received a new heart, he has been united to the person of Jesus Christ and his life is inevitably transformed. He has a new life. There is no such thing as a Christian whose life has not been changed. A changed life is the evidence that a work of grace has been effected in the heart. It is the witness of the Spirit to an individual that he is a child of God.

The questions of particular interest to us in this study are these: What is the nature of this life? When the Holy Spirit does a work of grace in the heart of an individual, what changes take place and how do those changes manifest themselves in the life? What is the nature of true spirituality?

These are very important questions for there are many different emphases in our day with respect to spirituality and the life of the Spirit. For some, the vital evidence of the indwelling of the Spirit is the possession of certain gifts. Others emphasize conformity to external standards of behaviour; others emphasize involvement in activities, ministry or the accruing of biblical knowledge.

There is certainly nothing wrong with spiritual activities. Bible study and ministry to others are important as are spiritual gifts and the duty of following one's moral convictions. But none of these things is in and of itself a gauge of spiritual life or a proof of the indwelling of the Holy Spirit. Sadly, Christianity in our day has fallen prey to patterns of thinking which are more cultural than biblical. We have come to equate spirituality with the fulfilment of roles – with preaching, witnessing, evangelizing, or with going through the motions of spiritual activities. But this kind of thinking is foreign to the Word of God. For the fact is that an individual can be a preacher, a teacher, a missionary; he can study the

Bible diligently and acquire an encyclopaedic knowledge; he can know the original languages and hold impeccable doctrinal beliefs; he can spend many hours in intense labour in evangelism and yet, for all this, still not be a Christian.

This is not to say that knowledge or evangelism are unimportant or that preachers, teachers and missionaries are not generally spiritual people. What I am saying is that these things of themselves do not guarantee that a person is a Christian.

For a number of years I was involved in leading discipleship groups in a local church. These met together once a week for approximately two years and they emphasized the activities of 'quiet time', Bible reading, Bible study, Scripture memory, evangelism, fellowship and prayer. Each week individuals would mark off a check-list of these activities as they completed them and we held one another accountable for faithfulness in doing these things. These are all good activities. But after some time I realized that the discipline of doing these activities does not mean that one is a spiritual person. A person is not spiritual because he can check off a list of activities. External actions in themselves are no evidence that a man or woman is indwelt by the Holy Spirit and is born again. And yet, let it be remembered, a truly spiritual person *will* be involved in such activities.

If this is true, how are we to define the nature of true spirituality? What is the essence of real Christianity? The answer, quite simply, is the life of Jesus. His life is the pattern of what is truly spiritual. We desperately need to come back to the example of his life as a revelation to us of the true nature of the Christian life. The entire life of the Lord Jesus Christ from his conception to his resurrection was lived in the power of the Holy Spirit (*Lk. 1:35; 4:1, 14, 18; Mt. 12:28; 1 Tim. 3:16; Heb. 9:14*). The same Holy Spirit who dwelt in Jesus dwells in every true Christian, and therefore the life that he communicates to and lives through a believer will bear real though imperfect resemblance to the life of Christ.

Jesus lived perfectly as God intended life to be lived by man. As one studies his life, recorded in the Gospels, one discovers that it was governed by a number of major principles from which he never deviated. He is the supreme example and pattern to us of what the Christian life is and how it is to be lived. This is why the Word of God exhorts us to look to Jesus and follow his example (*cf. Heb. 3:1–2; 12:3; 1 Pet. 2:20–22; Eph. 5:1*).

True Christianity, therefore, is to be seen in conformity to Christ, portrayed for us in the four Gospels and in the Epistles. J. C. Ryle says: 'Christ will never be found the Saviour of those who know nothing of following His example. Saving faith and real converting grace will always produce some conformity to the image of Jesus.'[2] This means that a person who is indwelt by the Spirit of God will manifest in his or her life the same spirit and the same life that was characteristic of the Lord Jesus Christ. If a person truly knows Christ, the principles that dominated the Saviour's life will dominate his. The values that Christ held he is going to hold; the passion of Christ's heart, in some measure, is going to be the passion of his heart. For, as we have said, when a person is regenerated by the Holy Spirit, he is united to the person of Jesus Christ whose life then begins to manifest itself in and through that individual.

This is why Paul can say in Galatians 2:20, 'I have been crucified with Christ; and it is no longer I who live, but Christ lives in me; and the life which I now live in the flesh I live by faith in the Son of God, who loved me, and delivered Himself up for me.' There was a point in time when Paul received a new life. Now the living Christ by his Spirit dwells in him. Consequently the life that is seen in Paul is really the life of Jesus by

[2] J. C. Ryle, *Holiness*, (Cambridge: James Clarke, reprinted 1956), p. 28.

the Spirit. It is still Paul who lives that life, but it is now being conformed to the likeness of Christ. And this is true for every Christian. This means that if Jesus actually dwells in a person, then his life will manifest itself. As Jesus once walked this earth as a man, so the believer will now walk, governed by the same principles, values, attitudes and objectives that governed Christ's life. This is precisely what 1 John 2:6 tells us: 'The one who says he abides in Him ought himself to walk in the same manner as He walked.' R. C. H. Lenski, the New Testament Greek scholar, makes the following comment on this verse:

> John says that the one making the true claim of union with God, is under obligation because of this claim, because of this abiding union with God, ever himself to walk just as that One did walk when he was here on earth. The walk or conduct of Jesus is the model for everyone who claims that he is in union and fellowship with God. He will follow in Jesus' steps.[3]

If we say we know Jesus Christ, then in some measure that which characterized his life is going to characterize ours. Note 1 John 2:29, 'If you know that He is righteous, you know that everyone also who practices righteousness is born of Him.' Jesus Christ was and is righteous. Therefore, those who know him will be righteous. This principle is reiterated in 1 John 3:5, 6: 'In Him there is no sin. No one who abides in Him sins; no one who sins has seen Him or knows Him.' There is a direct correlation between the believer and Christ. If we truly know him then to some extent his image will be seen in our lives because he dwells in us.

This leads us quite naturally to another question: How did Jesus live? What were the principles, values, attitudes, and objectives that governed his life? It is important that we ask

---

[3]R. C. H. Lenski, *The Interpretation of the Epistles of St. Peter, St. John and St. Jude*, (Minneapolis: Augsburg, 1966), p. 410.

these questions, for as we have said, the life that is truly spiritual is a distinctive *kind* of life, governed by definite and unalterable principles.

It is a sad fact that it is possible to engage in much activity that we consider to be spiritual and do it all in vain, as Christ indicated. On one occasion he stood before the scribes and Pharisees, the religious leaders of his day. They were orthodox, conservative and zealous; they had memorized the Word of God and they revered it. But Jesus said to them: 'This people honors Me with their lips, but their heart is far away from Me. But in vain do they worship Me . . .' (*Mk.* 7:6–7). What terrible words! In vain they worshipped God. It was not that they failed to 'worship'. They went to great lengths to worship and serve God. But everything they did and lived for was in vain because something foundational was absent from their hearts. It is imperative that we heed our Lord's warning.

The life of Jesus was not a vain life. He was a perfect man. When we look at his life and observe what he says about himself, and read the Scripture record of how he lived, it becomes very clear that his life was dominated by certain principles, all of which are of vital importance. In the next chapter we will see that there is one great undergirding principle which is foundational to all the others. It is absolutely imperative that we understand it, because it is the essence of true Christianity, and one of the major evidences that the Holy Spirit has regenerated us and indwells our hearts. Apart from this there simply is no Christianity.

2: *Jesus Christ, the Perfect Man*

In order to understand how Jesus lived as a man and therefore to understand the Christian life, it is important that we understand his inner character. For it is what Christ *is* as a person that is the foundation for all that he *did*. He lived as he did because he was first of all a certain *kind* of person. In Philippians 2:5–7, the apostle Paul makes the following statements about Jesus taking a human nature to himself, 'Have this attitude in yourselves which was also in Christ Jesus, who, although He existed in the form of God, did not regard equality with God a thing to be grasped, but emptied Himself, taking the form of a bond-servant, and being made in the likeness of men.' Paul uses the word 'form' (*morphē*) twice in this passage. It means the essence, the nature, or the innate character of a thing; that which is intrinsic and essential as opposed to that which is outward in appearance. When we are told in Philippians 2:6 that Christ existed in the *form* of God, it means that his innate character and nature, the essence of his being, is that of Deity. Jesus Christ is God. Then we are told in verse 7 that as God, Jesus took upon himself the nature and physical form of a man. In so doing, he became a certain kind of man; he took upon himself the *form* of a bondservant. This means that in his human nature, Jesus took upon himself the very nature, the inner disposition of a servant (*doulos*). What is the nature of Jesus as a man? He is a servant, a *doulos* of God. William Hendriksen makes these comments on this servant nature of Jesus:

THE CHRISTIAN

> Hence, he emptied himself *by taking* the form of a
> servant . . . Moreover, when he became a servant, he was
> not play-acting. On the contrary, *in his inner nature* (the
> *human* nature, of course) he became a servant, for we read,
> 'He took on *the form* of a servant.' . . . He, the sovereign
> Master of all, becomes servant of all. And yet, he remains
> Master.[1]

Jesus did not simply perform an act of serving. He actually
became a servant in nature. All that Jesus did, all that he
accomplished, flowed out of what he was by nature. The
character of Christ as a man is pre-eminently the character of
a servant.

In order to know what it means to say that the Lord Jesus
became a servant, we must understand how this word was
used in the culture to which Paul was writing. The Greek
word *doulos* is translated 'bond-servant' in our passage.
There are five different Greek words used in the New
Testament which have to do with being a servant. *Doulos*
meant the lowest form of servitude. It carries the idea of one
who gives himself wholly to another's will, to be totally
devoted to them in disregard of one's own personal interests.
G. Kittel's authoritative *Theological Dictionary of the New
Testament* makes the following comments with respect to the
word *doulos*:

> All the words in this group serve either to describe the
> status of a slave or an attitude corresponding to that of a
> slave . . . Where there is a [*doulos* slavery] human auto-
> nomy is set aside and an alien will takes precedence of one's
> own . . . The *doulos* has no right of personal choice . . .
> The word group serves to describe a relation of absolute
> dependence in which the total commitment of the *doulos*
> on the one side corresponds to the total claim of the *kurios*
> [lord] on the other . . . Alongside the will and commission

[1]William Hendriksen, *Philippians*, in *Philippians, Colossians and Philemon*,
(Grand Rapids: Baker, 1979; Edinburgh: The Banner of Truth Trust, 1981),
p. 109.

of the *kurios* there is no place for one's own will or initiative . . . Prominent in the theological use of the word group in the N[ew] T[estament] is the idea that Christians belong to Jesus as His *douloi* [slaves], and that their lives are thus offered to Him as the risen and exalted Lord.

The *doulos* has no will of his own, no independent life, since he is the property of his master. He lives to fulfil the will of another and to be totally dominated by the service, the interests and the desires of another. The words which would describe the life of such a servant would include dependence, submission, commitment and obedience. The Bible tells us that this is the life of Jesus. His heart-disposition and nature were that of a servant of God. This is the relationship that Jesus maintained with God. It is seen in many of the statements which he made with reference to himself, revealing his inner heart-longings, dispositions and attitudes. In such statements we see the controlling principles and motivations of his life, *what* he lived for and *how* he lived. The *how* of his living is as important for us to note as the objectives of his life.

In Matthew 11:29 the Lord Jesus gives us a description of his own spirit: he tells us what his heart is like. The other passages to which we will turn serve as illustrations of how this heart attitude was manifested. 'Take my yoke upon you, and learn of me; for I am meek and lowly in heart: and ye shall find rest unto your souls' (KJV). What is the essence of the heart of Jesus? We have seen that in Philippians 2 Paul describes his mind for us, but here we have his own description of himself: 'I am meek and lowly [humble] in heart.' He means, quite simply, that he is a servant and lives for the fulfilling of the will of another. This is what the words 'humility' and 'meekness' mean. A humble heart is a dependent heart and a meek heart seeks to live for the will of God in all circumstances regardless of the cost to itself. We see this attitude illustrated beautifully in the life of Jesus.

[17]

Other passages can be classified under five major headings:

I. JESUS LIVED FOR THE WILL OF GOD, NOT HIS OWN WILL

My food is to do the will of Him who sent Me, and to accomplish His work (*Jn. 4:34*).
I do not seek My own will, but the will of Him who sent Me (*Jn. 5:30*).
For I have come down from heaven, not to do My own will, but the will of Him who sent Me (*Jn. 6:38*).
I always do the things that are pleasing to Him (*Jn. 8:29*).
The cup which the Father has given Me, shall I not drink it? (*Jn. 18:11*).
For even Christ did not please Himself (*Rom. 15:3*).
Then I said, 'Behold, I have come (in the roll of the book it is written of Me) to do Thy will, O God' (*Heb. 10:7*).

II. JESUS LIVED FOR THE GLORY OF GOD

I do not receive glory from men (*Jn. 5:41*).
If any man is willing to do His will, he shall know of the teaching, whether it is of God, or whether I speak from Myself. He who speaks from himself seeks his own glory; but He who is seeking the glory of the one who sent Him, He is true, and there is no unrighteousness in Him (*Jn. 7:17–18*).
I honor My Father, and you dishonor Me. But I do not seek My glory; there is One who seeks and judges (*Jn. 8:49–50*).
If I glorify Myself, My glory is nothing, it is My Father who glorifies Me, of whom you say 'He is our God' (*Jn. 8:54*).
Now My soul has become troubled; and what shall I say, 'Father, save Me from this hour'? But for this purpose I came to this hour. 'Father, glorify Thy name' (*Jn. 12:27–28*).
Father, the hour has come; glorify Thy Son, that the Son may glorify Thee (*Jn. 17:1*).

I glorified Thee on the earth, having accomplished the work which Thou hast given Me to do (*Jn. 17:4*).

III. JESUS WAS A TOTALLY DEPENDENT MAN

Truly, truly, I say to you, the Son can do nothing of Himself, unless it is something He sees the Father doing; for whatever the Father does, these things the Son also does in like manner (*Jn. 5:19*).

I can do nothing on My own initiative. As I hear, I judge; and My judgment is just, because I do not seek My own will, but the will of Him who sent Me (*Jn. 5:30*).

My teaching is not Mine, but His who sent Me (*Jn. 7:16*).

I have many things to speak and to judge concerning you, but He who sent Me is true; and the things which I heard from Him, these I speak to the world (*Jn. 8:26*).

When you lift up the Son of Man, then you will know that I am He, and I do nothing on My own initiative, but I speak these things as the Father taught Me (*Jn. 8:28*).

For I did not speak on My own initiative, but the Father Himself who sent Me has given Me commandment, what to say, and what to speak. And I know that His commandment is eternal life; therefore the things I speak, I speak just as the Father has told Me (*Jn. 12:49–50*).

Do you not believe that I am in the Father, and the Father is in Me? The words that I say to you I do not speak on My own initiative, but the Father abiding in Me does His works (*Jn. 14:10*).

And Jesus, full of the Holy Spirit, returned from the Jordan and was led about by the Spirit in the wilderness (*Lk. 4:1*).

But if I cast out demons by the Spirit of God, then the kingdom of God has come upon you (*Mt. 12:28*).

IV. JESUS WAS A MAN UNDER THE AUTHORITY OF GOD

For I have come down from heaven, not to do My own will, but the will of Him who sent Me (*Jn. 6:38*).

As the living Father sent Me . . . (*Jn. 6:57*).

My teaching is not Mine, but His who sent Me (*Jn. 7:16*).
I have not come of Myself, but He who sent Me is true,
whom you do not know. I know Him; because I am from
Him, and He sent Me (*Jn. 7:28–29*).
He who sent Me is true (*Jn. 8:26*).
And He who sent Me is with Me; He has not left Me alone
(*Jn. 8:29*).
For I did not speak on My own initiative, but the Father
Himself who sent Me has given Me commandment, what to
say, and what to speak . . . therefore the things I speak, I
speak just as the Father has told Me (*Jn. 12:49–50*).
O righteous Father, although the world has not known
Thee, yet I have known Thee; and these have known that
Thou didst send Me (*Jn. 17:25*).

V. JESUS SERVED OTHERS

I am among you as the one who serves (*Lk. 22:27*).
For even the Son of Man did not come to be served, but to
serve, and to give His life a ransom for many (*Mk. 10:45*).
And when evening had come, after the sun had set, they
began bringing to Him all who were ill and those who were
demon-possessed. And the whole city had gathered at the
door. And He healed many who were ill with various
diseases, and cast out many demons (*Mk. 1:32–34*).
Jesus . . . rose from supper, and laid aside His garments;
and taking a towel, He girded Himself about. Then He
poured water into the basin, and began to wash the
disciples' feet, and to wipe them with the towel with which
He was girded (*Jn. 13:3–5*).
For you know the grace of our Lord Jesus Christ, that
though He was rich, yet for your sake He became poor,
that you through His poverty might become rich (*2 Cor.
8:9*).

Here we have set before us the life of the Lord Jesus Christ
and the reason why he was the man he was. He was a
bondslave of the living God and fulfilled to perfection

everything the word 'servant' signifies with respect to God and man. He did not exercise his will independently of his Father. He did not have plans of his own. He sought no life of his own. He did not make his own choices. He was a servant who lived totally for his Father. His one all-consuming passion was that his Father be glorified and his will be done in every area of his life. In one respect Jesus' life did not matter. That is, it did not matter to himself. The only thing that mattered was that God should be glorified. His life was devoid of the things this world highly esteems in terms of education, money, social standing or political influence. He was born in a stable to a peasant family and raised in a poor home in a despised village. His life was not dominated by ambition or self-promotion. He did not live for the fame and glory and praise of men. He lived for the kingdom of God and the interests of God. His only concern was the will of God and the glory of God.

Christ's life was also marked by a complete lack of independent action. His life was not self-directed but directed and empowered by the Holy Spirit. He did nothing on his own initiative. Jesus was merely a servant doing the will of God for God's sake. There is a total lack of 'self' in the Lord Jesus. But how different is the attitude or mindset which is characteristic of Satan! Selfishness is the very essence of the heart of Satan. Isaiah 14:13–15 gives us a brief insight into the inner heart-attitude that led to his fall:

> But you said in your heart, '*I will* ascend to heaven; *I will* raise my throne above the stars of God, and *I will* sit on the mount of assembly in the recesses of the north. *I will* ascend above the heights of the clouds; *I will* make myself like the Most High.'

The essence of Satan's heart-attitude is self-will, the promoting of his own will for his own sake. Five times here he says 'I will'. Satan's motivation is not God's will for God's glory but

THE CHRISTIAN

his own will for his own sake: '*I will* ascend; *I will* be exalted; *I will* be glorified; *I will* have a throne above all others.' Such is the essence of pride. Satan's desire is to be independent of God, autonomous and self-sufficient. Thus his fallen life was self-centred, self-directed and ambitious. It is the opposite of the mind of Christ. The One is selfless, humble and meek; the other is selfish, proud and ambitious.

Ever since the fall of man, when Satan breathed the poison of his pride into our hearts, this has been man's way. My will for my sake – independence of God, self-sufficiency and self-exaltation. This was our mindset by birth, it is the mindset of the world in which we live. It is that which characterizes the kingdom of Satan. But the Lord Jesus comes with another kingdom to deliver men from that which is of Satan, and to give them a new mind by giving them a new life, his own life. And his life is the life of a servant.

The salvation that Jesus brings to men is himself. To be saved involves becoming like Jesus, and that means a change of nature from being a proud, self-sufficient, self-centred person to becoming one who is a lowly, humble servant. This is what Jesus means when he tells us to take his yoke so that we might learn of him and become like him. That is how we too become meek and lowly of heart. When a person comes to faith in Jesus Christ, receiving a new heart through the regenerating work of the Holy Spirit, this is what he becomes, because this is what Jesus is. This is what Christianity is all about: lives being transformed into the image of Jesus Christ. This is the only sure evidence that the Holy Spirit has truly taken up residence in our hearts. In the next chapter we will look more closely at how this is accomplished.

3: *The Nature of True Conversion*

We have seen that the Word of God places great emphasis upon the servant heart. Such a heart is the very essence of a Christ-like life. We now need to understand that Christ's summons to enter the kingdom of God is a call to become servants of God. This is in fact the real meaning of true conversion, as Jesus makes clear in Mark 8:31–37.

> And He began to teach them that the Son of Man must suffer many things and be rejected by the elders and the chief priests and the scribes, and be killed, and after three days rise again. And He was stating the matter plainly. And Peter took Him aside and began to rebuke Him. But turning around and seeing His disciples, He rebuked Peter and said, 'Get behind Me, Satan; for you are not setting your mind on God's interests, but man's.'
>
> And He summoned the multitude with His disciples, and said to them, 'If anyone wishes to come after Me, let him deny himself, and take up his cross, and follow Me. For whoever wishes to save his life shall lose it; but whoever loses his life for My sake and the gospel's shall save it. For what does it profit a man to gain the whole world, and forfeit his soul? For what shall a man give in exchange for his soul?'

The Lord Jesus is here informing the disciples that he is going to suffer and be rejected and killed at the hands of the religious rulers. Peter takes the Lord aside out of genuine concern for him and begins to urge him to protect himself, to consider his personal safety: 'No, Lord, this will never happen to you.' But then Jesus turns around – you can almost see fire in his eyes – and he rebukes Peter. In so doing, he makes the astonishing statement: 'Get behind Me, Satan; for you are not setting your mind on God's interests, but man's' (*Mt. 16:22–3*).

First of all, Christ reveals the source of Peter's words; they come from Satan. Peter is being used by Satan to attempt to turn the Lord Jesus from the will of God by diverting him from the path of being a servant of God to one of self-interest. He should protect and save himself! The Lord pointedly responds that the issue revolves round two diametrically opposed mindsets. There is the setting of the mind on God's interests; alternatively there is the setting of the mind on self's interests. The mind set on self-interest is satanically inspired, while the mind set on God's interests is the mind of Christ. It is the mind of a servant.

Then Jesus gathers his disciples together along with the crowd; he has something of the utmost importance to say about what it means to follow him. His words are clear and penetrating in their meaning. The Lord begins by saying that if any one is determined to come after him, he is going to have to do three things: (1) Deny himself; (2) take up the cross; and (3) follow Christ. Then he adds, 'For whoever wishes to save his life shall lose it; but whoever loses his life for My sake and the gospel's shall save it.'

To understand what Jesus is saying, it is essential that we examine a number of key words and phrases to get their precise meaning. The Greek verb 'to follow' is *akolouthein*; it implies a commitment to be a disciple. In this context it means the committing of one's life unreservedly to the Lordship, rulership and authority of Jesus Christ. It means a decision to live for his will. But if we are to make this commitment Jesus says there are two things which must be done. Self must be denied and the cross must be taken up.

To deny self means to forget oneself. It is to disown one's self radically and completely. There must be a resolute turning from self and an end of living for self.

Then Jesus says we must take up a cross. Obviously he does not mean a literal, physical cross. He is speaking metaphorically. The 'cross' means death. In Roman times it was used as an instrument of execution. Here Jesus is referring specifically to a death to self, turning from ruling and controlling one's own life by personal ambition and self-interest, and a giving of oneself in total abandonment to Christ to live for him and follow him as Lord.

Immediately following these statements, Jesus gives a warning regarding what he has just said. It is imperative that we heed his words, for both obedience and disobedience have eternal consequences. First, he tells us the consequences of refusing to obey his words: 'For whoever wishes to save his life shall lose it.' The one seeking to save his life refuses to die to himself and to renounce living for himself; he refuses to submit his life to Jesus as Lord and to live for him. Jesus says that the individual who keeps himself as the centre of his life, will lose it. The word 'lose' in Greek means perish. It is used in John 3:16 ('For God so loved the world, that He gave His only begotten Son, that whoever believes in Him should not *perish*, but have eternal life') and means to die eternally. Jesus is dealing here with the issues of eternity. That becomes clear in the next verse where he says, 'For what does it profit a man to gain the whole world and forfeit his soul? For what shall a man give in exchange for his soul?' The issue here is that of salvation. Jesus is defining conditions for entering the kingdom of God.

R. C. H. Lenski brings out this point in his commentary on this verse:

This is not self-denial in the current sense of the word

but true conversion, the very first essential of the Christian
life . . . Self is thus cast out, and Christ enters in;
henceforth you live, not unto yourself, but unto Christ
who died for you.[1]

And William Hendriksen in commenting on the same verse
says:

We must be careful, however, not to conceive of this self-
denial, etc., in a chronological fashion, as if the Lord were
exhorting his hearers to practice self-denial for a while,
then after a lapse of time to take up and carry the cross,
and, once having shouldered that burden for another
time-period, to follow Jesus. The order is not chronological but logical. Together the three indicate *true
conversion*, followed by life-long *sanctification*.[2]

The person who seeks to save his life is contrasted with the
one who is prepared to lose his life for Christ's sake and the
gospel. That one, he says, will save his life.

We can, therefore, do one of two things with our life. We
can save it for ourselves or we can lose it, committing
ourselves unreservedly to Christ. The result of the latter will
be eternal salvation. Those who receive it give up a life
dominated by selfish interests for the sake of Another and his
interests, for the gospel represents the interests of God in this
world. Jesus is saying that there is a fundamental shift that
must take place in a man's life from self-rule to total
submission, from living for self-interest to living for God's
interests. His life must become dominated by the will of God
and by God himself. He no longer lives for his own sake.
Jesus now reigns as Lord. Self has been dethroned and that
life has one foremost concern, to live for the will and glory of

[1]R. C. H. Lenski, *Interpretation of St. Mark's Gospel*, (Minneapolis: Augsburg,
1961), p. 348.
[2]William Hendriksen, *The Gospel of Mark*, (Grand Rapids: Baker, 1975;
Edinburgh: The Banner of Truth Trust, 1976), p. 330.

God and to see his interests furthered in this world. Only such a person has experienced salvation.

Walter Chantry well expresses what is involved in self-denial and its relationship to the kingdom of God:

> Only one entrance may be found to the Kingdom of God. There is a narrow gate set at the head of the path of life. 'Strait is the gate, and narrow is the way, which leadeth unto life, and few there be that find it' (Matthew 7:14). No one with an inflated ego can squeeze through the door. There must be self-effacement, self-repudiation, self-denial even to become a disciple (a student) of Jesus Christ . . . Six times in the Gospels our great Prophet refers to his followers' taking up a cross. It was one of his favourite illustrations of self-denial . . .
>
> Some who call themselves 'Christian' in fact have never taken up their crosses. Being ignorant of the experience of self-execution, of self-denial, they are of necessity strangers to Christ. Our Lord himself intended his illustration and his demand to deepen alarm in such individuals . . . Without a cross there is no following Christ! And without following Christ there is no life at all! An impression has been given that many enter life through a wide gate of believing on Jesus. Then a few go through the narrow gate of the cross for deeper spiritual service. On the contrary, the broad way without self-denial leads to destruction. All who are saved have entered the fraternity of the cross.[3]

In the light of all that we have said about the word *doulos* (servant) involving denial of self and living for the will of another, it is obvious that what Jesus is saying here is that those who enter the kingdom of God must become servants of God. When a man becomes a Christian, he becomes a disciple or a follower, and a follower is a servant. A Christian

[3]Walter J. Chantry, *The Shadow of the Cross*, (Edinburgh: The Banner of Truth Trust, 1981), pp. 19–20, 22.

is therefore a servant of God, a *doulos* of God. How could it be otherwise? If Christianity implies Christ living in our lives, and the essence of his incarnate life is that of a servant, then his life in ours will be manifested as that of a servant. What Jesus is dealing with in these verses in Mark 8 is simply the nature of biblical repentance and true conversion.

We have seen that there are basically two master dispositions in existence in this world. There is the mind of Christ which is the mind of a servant and is characterized by selflessness; and there is the mind of Satan which is characterized by selfishness. One is controlled by the will of God and oriented towards God's interests; the other is controlled by self-will and oriented towards self's interests. Self-will is satanic in nature. It is the antithesis of the nature of Christ. Consequently when Jesus comes into our life, he changes our nature to conform to his own. This is accomplished when, by the grace of the Holy Spirit, we are brought to up to the fact that living for ourselves and ruling our own life is sin, and to turn from such a life by denying ourselves, taking up a cross and surrendering the whole of life to Jesus as Lord to become his follower or disciple. This is Jesus' open invitation to come out of the kingdom of Satan and to enter into the kingdom of God and become his servant. This truth is reiterated in many other parts of Scripture.

ROMANS 6:22

Paul says, 'But now having been freed from sin and enslaved to God, you derive your [fruit], resulting in sanctification, and the outcome, eternal life.' Note the phrase 'enslaved to God'. The word 'enslaved' is simply the verbal form of the word *doulos*. Having been freed from self-will, and having been brought into a relationship with God that is characterized by being his slave, there are certain results: 'You derive your [fruit], resulting in sanctification, and the outcome, eternal life.' If we are not servants we have not been freed from sin, and there will be no sanctified life, no fruit and no eternal life. Thus, this verse also shows us conclusively that the servant heart is the essence of true conversion and the foundation to a life of sanctification.

LUKE 14:25–27, 33

We live in a day when the conditions for discipleship have been relegated by many to an optional commitment which may come subsequent to one's conversion but does not have any bearing on one's eternal standing with God. Such teaching completely contradicts the Word of God. Discipleship or servanthood is *not* optional for a Christian and it most assuredly has direct bearing on one's eternal state. Note carefully the words of Jesus:

> Now great multitudes were going along with Him; and He turned and said to them, 'If anyone comes to Me, and does not hate his own father and mother and wife and children and brothers and sisters, yes, and even his own life, he cannot be My disciple. Whoever does not carry his own cross and come after Me cannot be My disciple . . . So therefore, no one of you can be My disciple who does not give up all his own possessions'.

Here Jesus is setting out specific conditions for becoming his disciple. He is not calling them, as Christians, to a deeper commitment. He is stating the conditions for entering the kingdom of God. Luke 14:27 contains similar words to Mark 8:34. While dealing with discipleship, it too speaks of the condition for conversion. This suggests that contextually the whole passage (*Lk. 14:25–33*) is dealing with conversion.

[29]

THE CHRISTIAN

The law of God reveals to us that we have been created to love the Lord our God with all our heart, soul, mind and strength and are to have no other gods before him (*Deut. 6:5; Ex. 20:3*). We were created by him and for him (*Col. 1:16*). He is to be the supreme love of our hearts. Our lives are to be submitted to him so that his will is to be the controlling principle of our lives. Thus, when Jesus sets forth these conditions for discipleship he is simply saying that if men are to enter the kingdom of heaven, they must return to the relationship they were originally created to fulfil. Jesus is defining biblical repentance. When he becomes the Lord and love of one's life, then God takes his rightful place in the heart of that individual, for Jesus is God.

According to Jesus' teaching, therefore, unless one becomes his love-servant, one cannot be a Christian, for that is what is involved in the repentance which is essential for salvation. J. I. Packer makes this point with great clarity:

> Repentance is more than just sorrow for the past; repentance is a change of mind and heart, a new life of denying self and serving the Saviour as king in self's place . . . More than once, Christ deliberately called attention to the radical break with the past that repentance involves. 'If any man will come after me, let him *deny himself*, and take up his cross daily, and follow me . . . whosoever will *lose his life for my sake*, the same (but only he) shall save it [Luke 9:23–24, cf. Luke 14:26, 33] . . . The repentance that Christ requires of His people consists in a settled refusal to set any limit to the claims which He may make on their lives.[4]

I THESSALONIANS I:9

When Paul reminds believers at Thessalonica how they became Christians, he speaks of how they 'turned to God from

[4]J. I. Packer, *Evangelism and the Sovereignty of God*, (Downers Grove: Inter-Varsity, 1961), pp. 71–72.

idols to *serve* a living and true God'. Their conversion, he says, was characterized by their turning from idols to become the servants (*doulos*) of God. Once again we come back to that same Greek word. This is always what characterizes a true conversion and new creation. If a man is not a servant he is not a new creation for he has never been changed. He is still the same person living under the dominion of sin or self.

THE PHARISEES

The Lord Jesus Christ was raised in a religious culture which had been the recipient of direct relevation from God. It possessed the Word of God. In Jesus' lifetime the Pharisees were the spiritual elite and were greatly revered by the common people. They were zealous, orthodox and biblically conservative. They tithed, prayed, fasted, spent hours in the temple and sought earnestly to convert Gentiles to the Jewish faith. Yet the most scathing words the Lord Jesus ever spoke were spoken against them. They serve as a very sober warning to us.

There was something fundamentally wrong with the Pharisees. Outwardly they appeared to be righteous, but Jesus had strong words to say to them from the prophet Isaiah, 'This people honors Me with their lips, but their heart is far away from Me. But in vain do they worship Me' (*Mt. 15:8–9*). The Pharisees had all the right words. They went through the motions of worshipping God. But Jesus tells us that it was all in vain, because their hearts were far away from God. Why? The Gospels give us the answer. Though these men were religious and outwardly moral, the driving force of their lives was self. Selfishness was the root motivation for all that they did. Self-will and self-exaltation were their dominant characteristics. They simply used their religion to promote themselves.

The Lord says this about these men: 'Woe to you, scribes and Pharisees, hypocrites! For you clean the outside of the cup and of the dish, but inside they are full of robbery and self-indulgence . . . Even so you too outwardly appear righteous to men, but inwardly you are full of hypocrisy and lawlessness' (*Mt. 23:25, 28*).

Christ says their hearts are full of self-indulgence and lawlessness. 'Lawlessness' is a key word for us to understand. In 1 John 3:4 we are told that 'sin is lawlessness'. Here we are given a definition of what sin is: lawlessness is the principle which underlies all sinful behaviour. Vine's *Expository Dictionary of New Testament Words* states that the word 'lawless' means the displacing of the will of God with the will of self. This was the kind of heart possessed by the Pharisees; a heart ruled by self which, as we have seen, is a satanic disposition. This is why Jesus told the Pharisees they were of their father the devil (*Jn. 8:44*). They were his children because they possessed his nature. Outwardly they were very religious, but inwardly their hearts had never been changed. Although physically circumcised they had never received what Paul calls a circumcised heart (*Rom. 2:29*). Consequently the entire bent of their lives was sinful. They thought they knew God and that their lives were pleasing to God but Jesus tells them that they were completely deceived.

This is a frightening warning to us. One of the great dangers for those raised in an evangelical Christian culture is the very danger that faced the Pharisees of Jesus' day. This is the lesson underscored in the words of Jesus: 'Not everyone who says to Me, "Lord, Lord," will enter the kingdom of heaven; but he who does the will of My Father who is in heaven. Many will say to Me on that day, "Lord, Lord, did we not prophesy in Your name, and in Your name cast out demons, and in Your name perform many miracles?" And then I will declare to them, "I never knew you; depart from Me, you who practice lawlessness"' (*Mt. 7:21–23*). There will be many in the day of judgment who will say to Christ, 'Lord, Lord', but to whom he will say, 'Depart from Me. I never knew you.' They are lost although they thought that they were saved. Notice that it says they call Jesus 'Lord'. They acknowledge his deity and lordship. They have used his name in their ministry; they have preached, cast out demons and performed many miracles all in the name of Jesus. But they are lost men and women. Why?

Some suggest that the reason these people are lost is that they are relying on works to give them acceptance with God rather than in the work of Jesus alone. Is this why they mention all the things they have done in his name? A careful reading of the passage indicates that these people are pointing to the success of their activities and ministries as proof that they must have been the children of God. They are not using their achievements as a basis for entering the kingdom of God, but assuming that their mighty works are proof that they already belonged to that kingdom. But Jesus says they are not genuine Christians because they *practise lawlessness*. This is the reason Jesus says they do not know him and why he tells them to depart from him. This is the same word we noted Jesus using to describe the heart of the Pharisees in Matthew 23 and which John describes as the root of all sinful behaviour. Jesus is saying that the bent of these people's lives is the practice of sin. Self is at the centre of their lives and has never been dethroned. They call Jesus 'Lord', they acknowledge him to be God, but they have never submitted their lives to him *as* Lord to become servants of God.

Who, then, does Jesus say will enter the kingdom of heaven? It is not those who *say* that he is Lord, but those who *do* the will of God. Who is the person who lives to do the will of God? He is a servant. Thus the person who is a true servant does not just acknowledge Jesus to be Lord, but actually submits to Jesus *as* Lord, to follow him and to do the will of

God. Such a person has turned from living for self and has given the whole of life to Jesus in order to live for him: 'He died for all, that they who live should no longer live for themselves, but for Him who died and rose again on their behalf' (*2 Cor. 5:15*).

It is a very sobering thing to realize that these men of whom Jesus speaks, though they were very busy in ministry and were doctrinally orthodox in the sense that they acknowledged his Deity and authority, yet were not doing the will of God. The heart that is dominated and controlled by self for selfish interests must be changed. It must be renounced and give way to a life totally surrendered to him as Lord and Saviour. It is no longer self but Jesus who is to be the centre of life. In other words, before an individual can live the Christian life, he must first of all be genuinely converted. And the Scriptures make it clear that the essence of a new heart which lies at the root of conversion is the heart of a servant.

When did you become a bondslave of Jesus Christ? When did you die to yourself and give yourself away to Jesus in order to live for God? The question is not how much biblical knowledge you possess, nor how active you are in ministry or other spiritual activities, nor even how orthodox are your beliefs. The issue is: Are we servants? Has our nature been changed? Are we a new creation? The proof that I am a Christian is not determined by what I profess but by how I live. This is the biblical test whether or not I am truly a child of God. Only a new nature which issues in a changed life is adequate proof of the presence of God's saving grace.

Jonathan Edwards points out the danger of having a sound knowledge of the Christian faith, yet lacking any experience of self-denial and wholehearted yielding to Christ:

In a *legal humiliation* men are made sensible that they are nothing before the great and terrible God, and that they

are undone, and wholly insufficient to help themselves . . . but they have not *an answerable frame of
heart*, consisting in a disposition to abase themselves, and
exalt God alone. This disposition is given only in *evangelical* humiliation, by overcoming the heart, and changing
its inclination . . . In a legal humiliation the conscience is
convinced . . . but because there is no spiritual understanding, the will is not bowed, nor the inclination
altered . . . In legal humiliation, men are brought to
despair of helping themselves; in evangelical, they are
brought voluntarily to deny and renounce themselves: in
the former they are subdued and brought to the ground; in
the latter, they are brought sweetly to yield, and freely and
with delight to prostrate themselves at the feet of God.

. . . Men may be legally humbled and have no
humility . . . be thoroughly convinced that they have no
righteousness, but are altogether sinful, exceedingly
guilty, and justly exposed to eternal damnation – and be
fully sensible of their own helplessness – without the least
mortification of the pride of their hearts . . . But the
essence of evangelical humiliation consists . . . in a mean
esteem of himself, as in himself nothing, and altogether
contemptible and odious . . . and . . . in denying his
natural self-exaltation, and renouncing his own dignity
and glory, and in being emptied of himself; so that he does
freely, and from his very heart, as it were renounce, and
annihilate himself. Thus the Christian doth in evangelical
humiliation.

. . . This is a great and most essential thing in true
religion. The whole frame of the gospel, every thing
appertaining to the new covenant and all God's dispensa-
tions towards fallen men, are calculated to bring to pass
this effect. They that are destitute of this, have no true
religion, whatever profession they may make, and how
high soever their religious affections . . . God has abundantly manifested in his word, that this is what he has a
peculiar respect to in his saints and that nothing is
acceptable to him without it . . . As we would therefore

[35]

make the Holy Scriptures our rule, in judging of . . . our own religious qualifications and state; it concerns us greatly to look at this humiliation, as one of the most essential things pertaining to true Christianity.[5]

We must come back to the foundations. We must start where God starts so that our lives are brought into conformity with his Word. The ultimate issue is: Are we servants? Have we experienced the change of heart the Holy Spirit produces when he effects the miracle of regeneration? Are we truly converted?

[5]*The Works of Jonathan Edwards*, Volume I, pp. 294–295.

4: *The Glory of God*

When the Holy Spirit takes up residence in our lives at regeneration, and unites us to Jesus Christ, monumental changes take place in our lives. Our hearts become like that of the Lord Jesus in nature in that they become servant hearts. But in addition to this, the overall life also becomes like that of the Lord Jesus in that the major principles which dominated his life now become characteristic of ours too.

The servant heart manifests itself in very specific ways with respect to God and man. As we have seen in Romans 8:5–7 the Christian is a spiritual man who walks in the Spirit and minds the things of the Spirit as opposed to walking in the flesh and minding the things of the flesh. This involves a radical transformation. Whereas life at one time was self-absorbed and self-centred, it is now consumed with God and his interests. There is no such thing as a life that has been indwelt by the Holy Spirit which does not manifest the reality of that fact in a passionate love for God and the things of God.

I use the word 'passionate' purposefully to indicate that this work is one which affects, in a dramatic way, the entirety of a man's being – his mind, will and emotions. True conversion is not a cold, dispassionate, half-hearted identification with spiritual things. It is a transformation of heart and life which results in the life being characterized by love in both emotional and volitional senses. The changed heart now burns with a longing, desire and zeal it never had before. Jonathan Edwards again makes this point in a marvellous passage in his discussion of the nature of true conversion. It is worth quoting at length:

> True religion consists, in a great measure, in vigorous and lively actings of the *inclination* and *will* of the soul, or the fervent exercises of the *heart*. That religion which God requires, and will accept, does not consist in weak, dull, and lifeless wishes, raising us but a little above a state of indifference. God, in his word, greatly insists upon it, that we be in good earnest, *fervent in spirit*, and our hearts vigorously engaged in religion: Rom. xii. 11. 'Be ye fervent in spirit, serving the Lord' . . . Deut. vi. 4, 5. 'Hear, O Israel, the Lord our God is one Lord: and thou shalt love the Lord thy God with all thy heart, and with all thy soul, and with all thy might.' It is such a fervent, vigorous engagedness of the heart in religion, that is the fruit of a real circumcision of heart, or true regeneration, and that has the promises of life: Deut. xxx. 6. 'And the Lord thy God will circumcise thine heart, and the heart of thy seed, to love the Lord thy God with all thy heart, and with all thy soul, that thou mayest live.'
>
> If we be not in good earnest in religion, and our wills and inclinations be not strongly exercised, we are nothing. The things of religion are so great, that there can be no suitableness in the exercises of our hearts, to their nature and importance, unless they be lively and powerful. In nothing is vigour in the actings of our inclinations so requisite, as in religion; and in nothing is lukewarmness so odious. True religion is evermore a powerful thing; and the power of it appears, in the first place, in its exercises in the heart, its principal and original seat. Hence true religion is called the *power of godliness*, in distinction from external appearances, which are *the form* of it, 2 Tim. iii. 5 . . . The Spirit of God, in those who have sound and solid religion, is a Spirit of powerful holy affection; and therefore, God is said 'to have given them the Spirit of power, and of love, and of a sound mind,' (2 Tim. i. 7). And such, when they receive the Spirit of God

in his sanctifying and saving influences, are said to be 'baptized with the Holy Ghost, and with fire;' by reason of the power and fervour of those exercises which the Spirit of God excites in them, and whereby *their hearts*, when grace is in exercise, may be said to *burn within them*. (Luke xxiv. 32.)

The business of religion is, from time to time, compared to those *exercises*, wherein men are wont to have their hearts and strength greatly exercised and engaged; such as running, wrestling, or agonizing for a great prize or crown, and fighting with strong enemies that seek our lives, and warring as those that by violence take a city or kingdom. Though true grace has various degrees, and there are some who are but babes in Christ, in whom the exercise of the inclination and will towards divine and heavenly things, is comparatively weak; yet every one that has the power of godliness, has his inclinations and heart exercised towards God and divine things with such strength and vigour, that these holy exercises prevail in him above all carnal or natural affections, and are effectual to overcome them: for every true disciple of Christ 'loves him above father or mother, wife and children, brethren and sisters, houses and lands; yea, more than his own life.' Hence it follows, that wherever true religion is, there are vigorous exercises of the inclination and will towards divine objects.[1]

Love to God is the result of true conversion. How that will be lived out in a practical sense in one's relationship with God can best be summed up in Deuteronomy 13:4, 'You shall follow the Lord your God and fear Him; and you shall keep His commandments, listen to His voice, serve Him, and cling to Him.' The person who is truly indwelt by the Holy Spirit will fulfil the spirit of this verse. In this chapter and the ones to follow we will look in detail at how love for God manifests itself in practical ways in the life of a true believer.

When the Lord Jesus Christ called men to respond to the

[1]*The Works of Jonathan Edwards*, Volume 1, pp. 237–238.

gospel, he called them to give themselves in total surrender and abandonment to him that they might become his followers and live for his sake. 'If anyone wishes to come after Me, let him deny himself, and take up his cross, and follow Me. For whoever wishes to save his life shall lose it; but whoever loses his life *for My sake* and the gospel's shall save it' (*Mk. 8:34–35*). The phrase 'for my sake' summarizes the essential motive of the Christian life, and underlines the absolute contrast between those who are Christians and those who are of the world. Those who are indwelt by the Holy Spirit live for Christ's sake. Their great passion is to glorify God. Christians see this as the ultimate objective of all of life and of their own life in particular.

Although this truth pervades the Scriptures it has all but been lost to the men and women of this generation. We live in a day in which secular humanism flourishes and much of its philosophy has crept into the church. Christianity today, generally speaking, is far removed from true biblical Christianity. The emphasis has become self-centred rather than God-centred both in the preaching of the gospel and in overall teaching on the Christian life. From much of the teaching that one hears today, one could conclude that God exists for man's sake, rather than man existing for God's sake. Yet the Scripture is emphatic that man was made for God, and understanding that purpose has a direct bearing on our view of the gospel and the Christian life. If we are wrong on the foundation, we will be wrong in everything that we attempt to build on it.

Men need to understand that they have been created to glorify God. The gospel when rightly proclaimed emphasizes that truth. Whenever the Holy Spirit effects the new birth, its outworking will be a life lived for the glory of God. Consequently we cannot rightly understand the gospel and the work of redemption unless we first of all start with God as the personal creator of all that exists and to whom all men are morally accountable. The gospel does not start with 'Jesus', but with God.

> The first need of man is summed up in the ancient admonition, 'Remember your Creator' (Eccles. 12:1) – that is to say, 'Acknowledge your creatureliness and give God the honor that belongs to him alone.' To understand the beginning is to understand the end, for the end is in the beginning, and to lose the beginning is to lose the end also and the whole meaning of things by which the end is bound to the beginning.
>
> The key to the mystery of existence is present in the opening words of Holy Scripture: 'In the beginning God.' We must start with God or we do not start at all in our comprehension of reality.[2]

The Scriptures teach us that in all that God does, he himself is the ultimate end in all his works. We see this first of all with respect to certain statements which God has made regarding himself:

> Thus says the Lord, the King of Israel and his Redeemer, the Lord of hosts: 'I am the first and I am the last, and there is no God beside Me' (*Is. 44:6*).
> Listen to Me, O Jacob, even Israel whom I called; I am He, I am the first, I am also the last (*Is. 48:12*).
> 'I am the Alpha and the Omega,' says the Lord God, 'who is and who was and who is to come, the Almighty' (*Rev. 1:8*).

Once more Jonathan Edwards provides us with wise commentary:

> God . . . is the *first cause* of all things [and] the supreme and *last end* of all things . . . When God is so often spoken of as the *last*, as well as the *first*, the *end* as well as the *beginning*, it is implied, that as he is the first, efficient cause and fountain, from whence all things originate; so, he is

[2]Philip E. Hughes, *Hope for a Despairing World*, (Grand Rapids: Baker, 1977), p. 43.

the last, final cause for which they are made; the final term to which they all tend in their ultimate issue.[3]

That which is uppermost in the mind of God is his glory. He is determined that his creation will give him the glory that is his right. 'For My own sake, for My own sake, I will act; for how can My name be profaned? And My glory I will not give to another' (*Is. 48:11*). Over and over again Scripture tells us that all things that exist were made for God; that all things come from him and are sustained by him for his glory:

> For by Him all things were created, both in the heavens and on earth, visible and invisible, whether thrones or dominions or rulers or authorities – all things have been created by Him and for Him. And He is before all things, and in Him all things hold together (*Col. 1:16–17*).
> The Lord hath made all things for himself (*Prov. 16:4*, KJV).
> For from Him and through Him and to Him are all things. To Him be the glory forever. Amen (*Rom. 11:36*).
> For it was fitting for Him, for whom are all things, and through whom are all things . . . (*Heb. 2:10*).
> Worthy art Thou, our Lord and our God, to receive glory and honor and power; for Thou didst create all things, and because of Thy will they existed, and were created (*Rev. 4:11*).

Scripture tells us that the Lord is worthy to receive all glory because he is the creator of all that exists, and he has the right to receive glory from that which he has created and sustains in existence. Man is a being who is kept in life by a loving creator. All his faculties, his life-breath and all the provisions for life are a gift from God. Thus the ultimate purpose for man is to live for the glory of God.

This is made especially clear to us in the great example of the life of the Lord Jesus Christ. As God's servant, the master principle which controlled his entire life and governed

[3]*The Works of Jonathan Edwards*, Volume 1, p. 106.

everything that he did, was God's glory. Various passages give us profound insight into the motivations of his heart and the objectives of his life:

> But when it was now the midst of the feast Jesus went up into the temple, and began to teach. The Jews therefore were marveling, saying, 'How has this man become learned, having never been educated?' Jesus therefore answered them, and said, 'My teaching is not Mine, but His who sent Me. If any man is willing to do His will, he shall know of the teaching, whether it is of God, or whether I speak from Myself. He who speaks from himself seeks his own glory; but He who is seeking the glory of the one who sent Him, He is true, and there is no unrighteousness in Him' (*Jn. 7:14–18*).

Jesus specifically states that his teaching did not originate with him. He was seeking the glory of the one who sent him rather than his own glory. Now Jesus knew that he was to receive glory and that the Father was going to exalt him. He longed to return to the glory which he had with the Father before his incarnation. As God, he had a right to be glorified and to seek glory, but as a man, Jesus also sought to bring glory to God alone. We see this in John 13:31–32, 'Now is the Son of Man glorified, and God is glorified in Him; if God is glorified in Him, God will also glorify Him in Himself, and will glorify Him immediately.' Similarly in John 17:1 Jesus prays, 'Father, the hour has come; glorify Thy Son, that the Son may glorify Thee.' Jesus desires to be glorified, not only because it is his innate right as God, but also so that he might in turn bring glory to his Father.

That the glory of God was uppermost in the mind of Jesus and was his ultimate aim in life is further seen in John 17:4, 'I glorified Thee on the earth, having accomplished the work which Thou hast given Me to do.' This was *the* principle, the mainspring of his life; everything else was subordinate to it.

In every area of his life Jesus sought to glorify his Father by obeying his will. This is dramatically brought out in John 12:20–28, in Jesus' response to his approaching crucifixion. He says, 'Now My soul has become troubled; and what shall I say, "Father, save Me from this hour"? But for this purpose I came to this hour. "Father, glorify Thy name."' His response to the realization of all that the crucifixion will mean to him is not to ask his Father to save him from the hour, for he knows it is the will of God. The very reason for his coming to earth was that he might embrace the cross and, by thus doing the will of God, to bring glory to God by the redemption of a ruined race. His prayer therefore is, 'Father, glorify Thy name.'

This is the example set before us by Jesus, the perfect man. He provides the pattern for the Christian life. The glory of God was the purpose for his incarnate existence, the controlling principle of his life, the ultimate objective in all that he did.

In view of the statements of Scripture about the importance of the glory of God, we are able to see more clearly the nature of sin, the purpose of the gospel and the character of the Christian life. The essence of sin is that men do not live for the glory of God. Note the following Scripture:

> Yet you, his son, Belshazzar, have not humbled your heart, even though you knew all this, but you have exalted yourself against the Lord of heaven; and they have brought the vessels of His house before you, and you and your nobles, your wives and your concubines have been drinking wine from them; and you have praised the gods of silver and gold, of bronze, iron, wood and stone, which do not see, hear or understand. But the God in whose hand are your life-breath and your ways, you have not glorified (*Dan. 5:22–23*).

The indictment against King Belshazzar was that he did not live for the glory of the One who created him and kept him in existence. But all men stand guilty at this point, 'For all have sinned and fall short of the glory of God' (*Rom. 3:23*) Why?

Because 'All of us like sheep have gone astray, each of us has turned to his own way' (*Is. 53:6*) to live for self, rather than for God.

Jesus tells us that in the days before his return it will be just like the days of Noah and Lot:

> And just as it happened in the days of Noah, so it shall be also in the days of the Son of Man: they were eating, they were drinking, they were marrying, they were being given in marriage, until the day that Noah entered the ark, and the flood came and destroyed them all. It was the same as happened in the days of Lot: they were eating, they were drinking, they were buying, they were selling, they were planting, they were building; but on the day that Lot went out from Sodom it rained fire and brimstone from heaven and destroyed them all. It will be just the same on the day that the Son of Man is revealed (*Lk. 17:26–30*).

Jesus mentions eating, drinking, marriage, buying, selling, planting and building, all of which are legitimate human activities when pursued in the will of God. The problem is that these material things dominated the lives of those whom Jesus mentions in his prophecy; they lived for these things. Their own needs, pleasure, security, happiness and fulfilment were their concern rather than God and his glory. And God judges them for it.

But when God regenerates us, he reverses that kind of living. The call of God in the gospel is for repentance from a sinful way of life; it summons us to commit ourselves to him through Jesus Christ that we may find forgiveness and begin to live for his glory. This is the whole purpose of the gospel and salvation:

> And I saw another angel flying in midheaven, having an eternal gospel to preach to those who live on the earth, and to every nation and tribe and tongue and people; and he

said with a loud voice, 'Fear God, and give Him glory' (*Rev. 14:6–7*).

The great design in preaching the gospel, the great end in view, is to see men turn from their sinful ways to God to fear him and live for his sake. Thus when God does a work of redemption in re-creating men through the new birth, his ultimate purpose is for his glory:

> I will say to the north, 'Give them up!' And to the south, 'Do not hold them back.' Bring My sons from afar, and My daughters from the ends of the earth, everyone who is called by My name, and whom I have created for My glory, whom I have formed, even whom I have made (*Is. 43:6–7*).
>
> To grant those who mourn in Zion, giving them a garland instead of ashes, the oil of gladness instead of mourning, the mantle of praise instead of a spirit of fainting. So they will be called oaks of righteousness, the planting of the Lord, that He may be glorified (*Is. 61:3*).
>
> For consider your calling, brethren, that there were not many wise according to the flesh, not many mighty, not many noble; but God has chosen the foolish things of the world to shame the wise, and God has chosen the weak things of the world to shame the things which are strong, and the base things of the world and the despised, God has chosen, the things that are not, that He might nullify the things that are, that no man should boast before God. But by His doing you are in Christ Jesus, who became to us wisdom from God, and righteousness and sanctification, and redemption, that, just as it is written, 'Let him who boasts, boast in the Lord' (*1 Cor. 1:26–31*).

In all that God does he makes himself the ultimate end. The purpose of creation, let it be underlined, is the glory of God; the essence of sin is man's failure to live for God's glory. The foremost purpose in preaching the gospel is to call men to realize their sinfulness in this regard and to seek forgiveness and reconciliation through repentance and faith in Jesus

Christ. Only then can they begin to fulfil the purpose for which they were created, namely, to live for the glory of God.

Thus the ultimate purpose of the Christian life is the glory of God. This was the aim of the Lord Jesus, our perfect example, and the same aim must be ours: 'Whether, then, you eat or drink or whatever you do, do all to the glory of God' (*1 Cor. 10:31*). Those who are born again of the Spirit of God have this basic motivation deeply rooted in their being, for it is the fundamental motivation of the new heart. It is the desire that naturally belongs to a true servant.

What in practical terms does it mean to live for the glory of God? To put it in its simplest form it means we live for *his* sake, rather than for our own sake. We live to do his will in the practical details of our lives, conforming our lives to the way he has ordained that we should live. Matthew Henry expresses it in these words:

He that is joined to Christ, is one Spirit. He is yielded up to him, and is consecrated thereby, and set apart for his use, and is hereupon possessed, and occupied, and inhabited, by his Holy Spirit. This is the proper notion of a temple – a place where God dwells, and sacred to his use, by his own claim and his creature's surrender. Such temples real Christians are of the Holy Ghost . . . But the inference is plain, that hence we are not our own. We are yielded up to God, and possessed by and for God; nay, and this in virtue of a purchase made of us: *Ye are bought with a price*. In short, our bodies were made for God, they were purchased for him. If we are Christians indeed, they are yielded to him, and he inhabits and occupies them by his Spirit, so that our bodies are not our own, but his . . . in eating and drinking, and in all we do, we should aim at the glory of God, at pleasing and honouring him. This is the fundamental principle of practical godliness.[4]

[4]Matthew Henry, *A Commentary on the Whole Bible*, Volume 6, (Old Tappan: Revell), pp. 536, 559.

Thus, in practical terms, God is glorified by the whole-hearted surrender of ourselves to him, and by the doing of his will as it is revealed in his Word, on a day by day basis.

This has a great deal to say to us about the basic motivations of those who are committed to living for the glory of God. It means that God is put first; the Lord and his will become pre-eminent in the heart and our personal happiness becomes subservient to the will of God. Personal happiness is never the dominating motivation for a true Christian. His main concern is God's glory, no matter what the cost to himself. We see this very clearly when the Lord Jesus was contemplating his approaching crucifixion and was troubled in soul. Yet he did not pray for deliverance but for his Father to glorify his name. He was committed first and foremost to the will of God and to the glory of God, even though that meant terrible suffering. Personal happiness, contentment, self-fulfilment were not the primary motives of his heart. God is first, not himself, and his ultimate joy is found in doing the will of God: 'My food is to do the will of Him who sent Me, and to accomplish His work' (*Jn. 4:34*). Jonathan Edwards explains what this means for us in his comments on I Corinthians 6:20 ('For you have been bought with a price: therefore glorify God in your body'):

Here, not only is glorifying God spoken of, as what summarily comprehends the end of religion, and of Christ redeeming us; but the apostle urges, that inasmuch as we are not our own, we ought not to act as if we were our own, but as God's; and should not use the members of our bodies, or faculties of our souls, for ourselves, but for God, as making him our end. And he expresses the way in which we are to make God our end, viz. in making his *glory* our end. 'Therefore *glorify God* in your body and in your spirit, which are his.' Here it cannot be pretended that though Christians are indeed required to make God's glory their end; yet it is but as *subordinate* end, as subservient to their own happiness; for then, in acting chiefly and ultimately for their own-selves, they would use themselves more as their *own* than as God's; which is directly contrary to the design of the apostle's exhortation, and the argument he is upon; which is, that we should give ourselves as it were away *from ourselves to God*, and use ourselves as *his* and not our *own*, acting for his *sake* and not our *own sakes*.[5]

What Edwards is saying is that in order to live for the glory of God, our own personal happiness and fulfilment can never be the focal point or the dominating drive of our lives. We must become subservient to this higher objective, the glory of God, so that our lives are no longer self-centred but God-centred and God-focused.

Happiness, joy and peace are never found when they are sought as ends in themselves. They are the *by-products* of a life rightly related to God through Jesus Christ. My chief goal must be God himself, and not joy, peace or happiness. He must never become a means to my personal ends. God does give peace and joy and happiness, but it always comes as a result of walking with him and doing his will. We find this principle exemplified in the life of Jesus: 'Thou hast loved righteousness and hated lawlessness; *therefore* God, Thy God, hath anointed Thee with the oil of gladness above Thy companions' (*Heb. 1:9*). The 'therefore' here is very important for it shows us that the primary thing in Jesus' life was living a righteous life and the result was the experience of gladness or joy. It is the by-product of a life of holiness.

This cuts right at the heart of much of the gospel preaching one hears today. We have come to the point where the major emphasis is on the benefits of the Christian life rather than on the person of God and his glory. The appeal is to come to Jesus to find peace and security and happiness or success and

5 *The Works of Jonathan Edwards*, Volume 1, p. 109.

prosperity. It is as if God were our servant and were here for us. But this is a distortion of the biblical message. The Bible begins with God and his glory, and with man as a bankrupt sinner who must repent of his sin by bowing at the feet of Jesus Christ to live for the glory of God. This the true Christian has done, and continues to do throughout his days on this earth, recognizing that God is a sovereign God, and that when he effects a work of salvation he does so for his glory. The same Holy Spirit who indwelt the life of Jesus Christ indwells the life of every child of God, and manifests his presence by bringing that redeemed life into conformity with the life of Christ. That life was pre-eminently concerned with the glory of God; ours should be too.

5: *The Life of Worship*

A major characteristic of love for God and one of the essential foundations for glorifying God is a worshipping heart and life. Those who are redeemed by the blood of the Lamb and regenerated by the Holy Spirit become worshippers of the living God. This is one of the leading marks of those whom the Bible describes as being 'saved'. As Paul says, 'for we are the true circumcision, who worship in the Spirit of God and glory in Christ Jesus and put no confidence in the flesh' (*Phil. 3:3*). In a very real sense a man is saved to worship. It is our ultimate priority.

By 'worship' I do not mean only a corporate assembly that meets together once or twice a week in what is commonly referred to as a worship service, although that is involved. Such meetings and other activities are very important as expressions of true worship. But worship is not primarily an action as much as a state of spirit which is foundational to the activities of worship. True worship involves the entirety of one's life every day of the week. It cannot be confined to something that happens only on one or two hours in the week. True worship is a way of life.

A worshipping life is the central expression of our response to the revelation of God to our hearts. It is directly related to a proper understanding of the gospel and of what it means to live for God's glory. Worship is selfless giving to God, and begins at the point an individual receives a new heart in regeneration and becomes a servant of God. At that point the life is wholly surrendered to live for his sake and for his glory.

Worship is not simply a matter of speaking or singing certain words or going through the motions of religious activity as Jesus makes clear in speaking to the Pharisees: 'This people honors Me with their lips, but their heart is far away from Me. But in vain do they worship Me . . .' (*Mt. 15:8–9*). Words are meaningless apart from a right heart.

In the Old Testament the Lord makes it clear that acceptable worship involves much more than fulfilling a prescribed religious activity or ritual: 'I hate, I reject your festivals, nor do I delight in your solemn assemblies. Even though you offer up to Me burnt offerings and your grain offerings, I will not accept them; and I will not even look at the peace offerings of your fatlings. Take away from Me the noise of your songs; I will not even listen to the sound of your harps. But let justice roll down like waters and righteousness like an ever-flowing stream' (*Amos 5:21–24; cf. Is. 1:11–15*).

True worship is not a matter of being in a certain place and saying certain words; it is not a matter of form, but of being in a right relationship with God. 'God is spirit, and those who worship Him must worship in spirit and truth' (*Jn. 4:24*). That is, worship must involve our whole hearts and be consistent with and conform to the revealed Word of God. We must worship God as he has revealed himself in his Word, with our dependence on his acceptance based solely on the blood atonement of Jesus Christ. There must be both spirit and truth or our worship is unacceptable to God. William Hendriksen comments as follows on Jesus' words:

> The final phrase *in spirit and truth* has been interpreted variously. The context should decide. Jesus has been emphasizing two things: a. worship which is worth the name is not hampered by *physical* considerations; e.g., whether one prays at this place or at that place (4:21); and b. such worship operates in the realm of *truth*: clear and definite knowledge of God derived from his special revelation (4:22). In such a setting, it would seem to us,

worshiping *in spirit and truth* can only mean a. rendering such homage to God that the entire heart enters into the act, and b. doing this in full harmony with the truth of God as revealed in his Word. Such worship, therefore, will not only be spiritual instead of physical, inward instead of outward, but it will also be directed to the true God as set forth in Scripture and as displayed in the work of redemption . . . Genuine worshipers worship *in spirit and truth*![1]

Worship begins with the heart, in the total giving of ourselves to God. This is why an understanding of the servant heart and true conversion are so important. Apart from a servant heart no man can worship God acceptably, for as Jesus says, 'his heart is still far from him'. Acceptable worship starts with a surrendered heart. This echoes what was said in the previous chapter on the glory of God. To live for the glory of God is to live for his sake. It is to put him first, to make him pre-eminent. The natural outflow of that commitment is a *life* of worship. A worshipping life is primarily concerned with the honour and glory of God, with giving *to* God and with ministering *to* him. This is confirmed by the Greek words which are used to describe worship:

The New Testament uses several words for worship. Two of them particularly are noteworthy. The first is *proskuneō*, a commonly used term that literally means 'to kiss toward,' 'to kiss the hand,' or 'to bow down.' It is the word for worship used to signify humble adoration. The second word is *latreuō*, which suggests rendering honor, or paying homage. Both terms carry the idea of giving, because worship *is* giving something to God. The Anglo-Saxon word from which we get our English word is *weorthscipe*, which is tied to the idea of worthiness. Worship is ascribing to God His worth, or stating and affirming His supreme value.

[1]William Hendriksen, *The Gospel of John*, (Grand Rapids: Baker, 1953; Edinburgh: The Banner of Truth Trust, 1959), Volume I, p. 167.

When we talk about worship, we are talking about something *we* give to God. Modern Christianity seems committed instead to the idea that God should be giving to us. God *does* give to us abundantly, but we need to understand the balance of that truth – we are to render honor and adoration to God. That consuming, selfless desire to give to God is the essence and the heart of worship. It begins with the giving first of ourselves, and then of our attitudes, and then of our possessions – until worship is a way of life.[2]

GOD'S PURPOSE IN REDEMPTION

We are told in Scripture that the Lord Jesus came to this earth for a specific purpose: 'For the Son of Man has come to seek and to save that which was lost' (*Lk. 19:10*). John 4:23 further explains *why* Jesus seeks to save the lost: 'But an hour is coming, and now is, when the true worshipers shall worship the Father in spirit and truth; for such people the Father seeks to be His worshipers.' Worship has high priority with God for man was created to worship him. When anyone is reconciled to God, he becomes a true worshipper. This is the essence of our submission to God, as Jesus says in response to Satan's temptation, 'You shall worship the Lord your God, and serve Him only.' This is man's highest calling and priority. Men are redeemed that God might be glorified through worshipping lives.

The Christian's *primary* calling is not to service, ministry or evangelism. It is to worship, and from that worshipping life will flow a life of fruitful ministry and service. This is not to diminish the importance of service and ministry for these are vitally important duties by which one can and should express worship to God. But what cannot be over-emphasized is that a worshipping spirit is foundational to spiritual

---

[2]John MacArthur, Jr., *The Ultimate Priority*, (Chicago: Moody, 1983), p. 14.

activities. It is possible to be involved in the activities apart from having the right spirit. Service and ministry, even our own needs, must never be allowed to come first or to be our primary concern. God *himself* must come first as our Lord's teaching on prayer makes abundantly clear. His model prayer begins, 'Our Father who art in heaven, hallowed be Thy name' (*Mt. 6:9*). It teaches us what should be the first concern in our hearts. Martyn Lloyd-Jones comments:

> The important thing to grasp is this: that it matters not what our conditions and circumstances may be, it matters not what our work may be, it matters not at all what our desires may be, we must never start with ourselves, we must never start with our own petitions.

> That principle applies even when our petitions reach their highest level. Even our concern for the salvation of souls, even our concern for God's blessing upon the preaching of the Word, even our concern that those who are near and dear to us may become truly Christian, even these things must never be given the first place, the first position. Still less must we ever start with our own circumstances and conditions . . . Before we begin to think of ourselves and our own needs, even before our concern for others, we must start with this great concern about God and His honour and His glory. There is no principle in connection with the Christian life that exceeds this in importance.[3]

The Scriptures eloquently testify to the priority of worship in the Christian life. By command, by principle, by historical illustration from the nation of Israel and by the example of individual lives, the Bible repeatedly draws attention to this truth. From the Pentateuch to the book of Revelation, worship is a central motif. Man fell in Genesis, but with his final restoration, described in Revelation, we find him restored

---

[3] D. Martyn Lloyd-Jones, *Studies in the Sermon on the Mount*, Volume 2, (Grand Rapids: Eerdmans, 1960), p. 58.

to worship. Revelation 4 and 5 present a picture of the
activity of heaven. It centres around worship. Revelation 22
records the final restoration of all things and says, 'And there
shall no longer be any curse; and the throne of God and of the
Lamb shall be in it, and His bond-servants shall serve Him'
(*Rev. 22:3*). The word 'serve' is the same word translated
'worship' elsewhere. They shall worship him. The climax of
all history results in a redeemed people who worship their
God.

The book of Leviticus describes in great detail the proper
way to worship God. The people redeemed from the land of
Egypt, before they are taken into the land of promise where
they must war, are first taught how to worship God
acceptably. They cannot war unless they first of all worship.
Leviticus instructs the people in the *basis* for true worship, as
well as the *conditions* which must be met. Worship was
central to the life of the nation.

In the Old Testament, worship covered all of life; it was
the focus of the people of God . . . All the political, social,
and religious activity in Israel revolved around the law,
and critical to the law was the list of ceremonial offerings
described in Leviticus 1–7, all of which are acts of
worship. The first offering on the list is the burnt offering,
which was unique because it was completely consumed –
offered totally to God. No part was shared either by the
priests or by the offerer, as in other offerings. The burnt
offering was the most significant illustration of worship. In
fact, the altar on which all the offerings were given was
known as the altar of the burnt offering. Whenever the
offerings are referred to in the Scripture, the burnt
offering appears at the beginning of the list, because when
anyone comes to God he is to come first of all in an act of
worship, where all is given to God. Thus God reinforced
worship as the priority.[4]

[4]John MacArthur, Jr., *The Ultimate Priority*, pp. 2–3.

Consequently the book of Psalms is full of the call to worship:

> O come, let us sing for joy to the Lord; let us shout joyfully to the rock of our salvation. Let us come before His presence with thanksgiving; let us shout joyfully to Him with psalms. For the Lord is a great God, and a great King above all gods, in whose hand are the depths of the earth; the peaks of the mountains are His also. The sea is His, for it was He who made it; and His hands formed the dry land. Come, let us worship and bow down; let us kneel before the Lord our Maker (*Ps. 95: 1–6*).
>
> Sing to the Lord a new song; sing to the Lord, all the earth. Sing to the Lord, bless His name; proclaim good tidings of His salvation from day to day. Tell of His glory among the nations, His wonderful deeds among all the peoples. For great is the Lord, and greatly to be praised; He is to be feared above all gods. For all the gods of the peoples are idols, but the Lord made the heavens. Splendor and majesty are before Him, strength and beauty are in His sanctuary (*Ps. 96:1–6*).

Men are redeemed to worship. Both the Old and New Testaments herald the same call to worship. And the wonderful thing is that as a person cultivates the habit and discipline of consistent worship, it results in his being transformed into the image of Christ himself: 'But we all, with unveiled face beholding as in a mirror the glory of the Lord, are being transformed into the same image from glory to glory, just as from the Lord, the Spirit' (*2 Cor. 3:18*). The power of the gospel through the Spirit removes from our hearts the veil which hid the face of God. And now we are able to behold his glory in an open, face-to-face relationship. The Spirit brings the Word to our hearts and we worship in spirit and truth. This is the true source of the on-going transformation in the lives of Christians.

WHAT IS WORSHIP?

To worship God means to express love for him by adoration, reverence, thankfulness, praise, submission and obedience. It is to have our lives overwhelmed and consumed with the wonder, greatness and worthiness of his being and his works; it means a consciousness of his love which constrains a response of love for him. A. W. Tozer gives the following description of worship:

> Worship means 'to feel in the heart'; that's first – feel it in the heart . . . Worship also means to 'express in some appropriate manner' what you feel . . . And what will be expressed? 'A humbling but delightful sense of admiring awe and astonished wonder.' It is delightful to worship God, but it is also a humbling thing; and the man who has not been humbled in the presence of God will never be a worshiper of God at all . . . it's an attitude, a state of mind, a sustained act, subject to degrees of perfection and intensity . . . Worship . . . rises or falls with our concept of God . . . I believe we ought to have again the old Biblical concept of God which makes God awful and makes men lie face down and cry, 'Holy, holy, holy, Lord God Almighty' . . . Then there is *admiration*, that is, appreciation of the excellency of God . . . *Fascination* is another element in true worship. To be filled with moral excitement. To be captivated and charmed and entranced . . . with who God is, and struck with astonished wonder at the inconceivable elevation and magnitude and splendor of Almighty God . . . Next is *adoration*, to love God with all the power within us. To love God with fear and wonder and yearning and awe.[5]

As one studies the lives of those people in Scripture who had a revelation of the living God to their hearts, one thing

[5]A. W. Tozer, *Worship: The Missing Jewel in the Evangelical Church*, (Harrisburg: Christian Publications), pp. 8–9, 24–28.

stands out consistently in each case. They all became overwhelmed with the greatness, the goodness, the majesty and the holiness of God. And this in turn produced a deep sense of personal sinfulness and a concern to walk humbly with him.

When Moses approached God at the burning bush he was instructed to remove his shoes; the ground on which he stood was holy because of the presence of God. 'Then Moses hid his face, for he was afraid to look at God' (*Ex. 3:6*). That is reverence and humility.

When Isaiah received his vision of the Lord seated on his throne and the seraphim crying 'Holy, holy, holy is the Lord of hosts', he was suddenly struck with a painful realization of his sinfulness and cried out, 'Woe is me, for I am ruined! Because I am a man of unclean lips, and I live among a people of unclean lips; for my eyes have seen the King, the Lord of hosts' (*Is. 6:5*). This is always what happens. To know God is to sense our own unworthiness before him.

When Job was finally confronted by God his response was a significant one: 'I know that Thou canst do all things, and that no purpose of Thine can be thwarted. "Who is this that hides counsel without knowledge?" Therefore I have declared that which I did not understand, things too wonderful for me, which I did not know. "Hear, now, and I will speak; I will ask Thee, and do Thou instruct me." I have heard of Thee by the hearing of the ear; but now my eye sees Thee; therefore I retract, and I repent in dust and ashes' (*Job 42:2–6*). Job's response is one of humility and repentance. Similarly, in the book of Revelation, when the apostle John sees the risen and glorified Christ he says, 'And when I saw Him, I fell at His feet as a dead man' (*Rev. 1:17*).

When the Lord of glory reveals himself to men and women the response is always one of godly fear, a deep sense of sinfulness, reverence, awe, humility, repentance and submission. This is far removed from the superficial, flippant, casual and overly familiar approach to God that many take today. How grateful we should be that he is a God of love and grace! But have we forgotten that God is a God of light in whom there is no darkness at all, who is of such purity that he cannot look upon iniquity, and who judges sin? Those who are truly redeemed by the blood of Christ and have been brought to know God have a sense of godly fear and reverence in approaching him and in living before him. A true worshipper never takes sin lightly, but is careful to walk before God in a spirit of holiness, for only the man who walks in holiness can worship God acceptably: 'Who may ascend into the hill of the Lord? And who may stand in His holy place? He who has clean hands and a pure heart . . .' (*Ps. 24:3-4*).

The Christian realizes that he has boldness of access to God through the blood of Jesus and may come with a whole heart and sincere faith. But he is also conscious that he has this access only because of blood. That blood reminds us of God's holiness and wrath, of Christ's sacrifice, and of our own sin and unworthiness. It produces humility, reverence and a sober spirit, as well as confidence, boldness and love. God is love but he is also holy, and a true saint has an abiding appreciation for both aspects of his being.

True worship will focus primarily on two things: the wonders of the person and being of God himself and the greatness of his works. In one of the most beautiful psalms of worship, we find the following words:

> I will extol Thee, my God, O King; and I will bless Thy name forever and ever. Every day I will bless Thee, and I will praise Thy name forever and ever. Great is the Lord, and highly to be praised; and His greatness is unsearchable. One generation shall praise Thy works to another, and shall declare Thy mighty acts. On the glorious splendor of Thy majesty, and on Thy wonderful works, I will meditate (*Ps. 145:1-5*).

The psalmist goes on from this point to speak of the righteousness, goodness, mercy and sovereign power of God, emphasizing both who God is and what he has done. This same concept of worship is reiterated in Revelation 4 and 5 where the theme is the worthiness of both the Father and the Son as the saints bow down before the throne of God and cry out, 'Worthy art Thou, our Lord and our God, to receive glory and honor and power; for Thou didst create all things, and because of Thy will they existed, and were created' (*Rev. 4:11*). And then they fall down before the Lord Jesus Christ, the Lamb of God, and add, 'Worthy art Thou to take the book, and to break its seals; for Thou wast slain, and didst purchase for God with Thy blood men from every tribe and tongue and people and nation. And Thou hast made them to be a kingdom and priests to our God; and they will reign upon the earth . . . Worthy is the Lamb that was slain to receive power and riches and wisdom and might and honor and glory and blessing' (*Rev. 5:9–10, 12*).

The being of God – the fact that he is a sovereign Lord and creator, eternal and unchanging – elicits submission, praise and adoration. The character of God – his holiness and righteousness and justice, love, mercy, forgiveness, compassion and faithfulness – is the infinite source of all praise and adoration. His works of redemption expressed in the sending of his Son as the Lamb of God to die for a sinful race of men, led to this sure response. Redemption means that we will know God and enjoy him. What, then, can a Christian do but fall down at his feet in wonder, love, adoration and praise, saying, 'Such is God, our God forever and ever' (*Ps. 48:14*).

Worship is intimate, personal and deeply humbling. It is the desire of the heart to express love for God and to see him glorified; it is the desire to exalt him so that his name may be hallowed in our own hearts and in the hearts of others. That is why the Lord begins his instruction on prayer with worship (*Mt. 6:9*). In the same context he says, 'But you, when you pray, go into your inner room, and when you have shut your door, pray to your Father who is in secret, and your Father who sees in secret will repay you' (*Mt. 6:6*). This teaches us that worship is a vital part of prayer and must be cultivated by meditation and by being quietly alone with God. There simply is no substitute for this. True worship begins by being shut up in secret with God and it moves out from there to encompass the entirety of one's life. It is something which is very intimate and very personal between an individual believer and his God. But such a life requires making choices that make worship and time alone with God the great priority of one's life. In our age of achievement and activity it is very easy to substitute service and ministry for being alone with God. But we need to heed the words of Jesus spoken to Martha as he gently rebuked her for criticizing her sister Mary who was seated at his feet listening to his word while she was involved in serving:

> Martha, Martha, you are worried and bothered about so many things; but only a few things are necessary, really only one, for Mary has chosen the good part, which shall not be taken away from her (*Lk. 10:41–42*).

THE EXAMPLE OF DAVID

Many of David's psalms are psalms of worship. He is an extremely important figure in biblical history. Apart from that of Jesus himself, his life is recorded with greater detail than any other in the Word of God. There is a reason for this. David was a man after God's own heart and his life mirrors for us the spirit of a child of God. The Psalms reveal the motives and desires of David's heart. Psalm 27:4 expresses the major commitment and focus of his life: 'One thing I have asked from the Lord, that I shall seek: that I may dwell in the house of the Lord all the days of my life, to behold the beauty of the Lord, and to meditate in His temple.' This is commitment to a life of worship. David says that it is the *one thing* that he asked of the Lord and which he would seek after all the days of his life. The commentary of Keil and Delitzsch makes this comment:

> The future [tense] is used side by side with the perfect in ver. 4*a*, in order to express an ardent longing which extends out of the past into the future, and therefore runs through his whole life . . . A life-long dwelling in the house of Jahve, that is to say intimate spiritual intercourse with the God, who has His dwelling, His palace in the holy tent, is the one desire of David's heart, in order that he may behold and feast upon (. . . a clinging, lingering, chained gaze . . .), the pleasantness (or gracefulness) of Jahve, *i.e.* His revelation, full of grace, which is there visible to the eye of the spirit . . . [The house of the Lord] is a designation of the place consecrated to devotion, and [the word meditate] is meant to refer to contemplative meditation that loses itself in the God who is there manifest.[6]

A 'chained gaze' upon the God of glory and a feasting upon the pleasantness and gratefulness of his person and character! Such was the desire of David's heart. One thing was uppermost in his mind, and his life revolved around one major overriding commitment. W. S. Plumer comments:

> The meaning is, 'I have desired one thing preëminently, I have desired it so much that in comparison I have desired nothing else. And I have sought it religiously, devoutly, by prayer of the Lord; and I will never cease to desire it'.[7]

Joseph Carroll expresses it more fully:

> David's desire is an ardent longing that runs out of the past

[6]C. F. Keil and F. Delitzsch, *Commentary on the Old Testament*, Volume 5, *Psalms*, (Grand Rapids: Eerdmans, reprinted 1978), pp. 356–357.
[7]W. S. Plumer, *Psalms*, (Edinburgh: The Banner of Truth Trust, reprinted 1978), p. 354.

into the future. It is not a momentary thing. Intimate, spiritual intercourse is the one consuming desire of his heart; and it is this which dominated David all his days. Is that not surprising? David is a man's man, a great soldier, a king of kings; and what does he want to do? The one thing he wants is to behold the beauty and pleasantness of the Lord. Everything else is relatively incidental: being a great leader, being a great king, being a great preacher, being a great psalmist. Only one thing really matters – intimate fellowship with God. To be a true worshipper of God is his passion.[8]

Deep in the heart of every child of God is the desire to worship him. This is something the Spirit of God places within those who receive a new heart. As with David, a desire develops to dwell continually in God's presence, to contemplate his glory and goodness, and to yield to him in submission, love and devotion. A new longing arises for a life directed towards the Lord in praise and adoration for what he is in himself. All of this involves a giving of oneself and all that one has to him for his sake in response to all that he is and all that he has done for us.

This is graphically illustrated in the life of the Mary who anointed the Lord Jesus prior to his crucifixion. She enters the room with a very expensive vial of perfume and simply pours the entire contents over his head, then bows at his feet and wipes his feet with her hair. She anoints his body for burial, aware of the fact that he is going to die. Therefore she comes to him in an act of extravagant, sacrificial love to minister to him. She is not seeking anything from him. In a totally selfless way she is giving herself to minister to her Lord. The money from the ointment could have been used to minister to the poor, but Mary puts Christ first and he commends her for it; and he adds that wherever the

[8]Joseph S. Carroll, *How to Worship Jesus Christ*, (Memphis: Riverside, 1984) p. 12.

gospel is preached what Mary had done would be remembered.

Jesus obviously placed very high value on Mary's action. It was very precious to him. Does this not tell us a great deal about priorities and true value in the Christian life? What Mary did wonderfully illustrates the heart of true worship. It is expressing love for God, in the giving of ourselves to him for his sake, for the innate worth of his being and his character and in response to the manifestation of his love to us. The principal motivation of a true Christian is to love and serve God, not from selfish interests, but from a selfless desire to see him glorified. Jonathan Edwards emphasizes this point in his discussion of the nature of the basic motivations of the new heart:

> It was before observed, that the affection of love is as it were the fountain of all affection; and particularly, that Christian love is the fountain of all gracious affections. Now the divine *excellency* of God . . . his works, ways, &c. is the primary reason, why a true saint loves these things; and not any supposed *interest* that he has in them, or any conceived benefit that he has received or shall receive from them . . . And as it is with the *love* of the saints, so it is with their *joy* and spiritual *delight*: the first foundation of it is not any consideration of their interest in divine things; but it primarily consists in the sweet entertainment their minds have in the contemplation of the divine and holy beauty of these things, as they are in themselves. And this is indeed the very main difference between the joy of the hypocrite and the joy of the true saint. The former rejoices in *himself*; self is the first foundation of his joy: the latter rejoices in *God* . . . The first foundation of the delight a true saint has in God, is his own perfection; and the first foundation of the delight he has in Christ, is his own beauty.[9]

[9]*The Works of Jonathan Edwards*, Volume I, pp. 275, 277.

This is but another way of saying that the heart of the true saint is a heart of worship. The believer has come to love God purely and simply for the worthiness of what he is in himself, or as David put it, for his beauty (*Ps. 27:4*). Thomas Watson has similar thoughts to those of Jonathan Edwards:

> Love to God must be pure and genuine. He must be loved chiefly for himself . . . We must love God, not only for his benefits, but for those intrinsic excellencies with which he is crowned. We must love God not only for the good which flows from him, but for the good which is in him. True love is not mercenary; he who is deeply in love with God, needs not be hired with rewards; he cannot but love God for the beauty of his holiness; though it is not unlawful to look for benefits. Moses had an eye to the recompense of reward (Heb. xi. 26); but we must not love God for his benefits only, for then it is not love of God, but self-love.[10]

Those who are truly born again and indwelt by the Holy Spirit worship God in spirit and truth. The Christian has dedicated his life to the glory of God and he loves him for his own sake with submission, adoration, praise and thanksgiving. But, as we shall see, this list of Christian characteristics is incomplete. Obedience is one of the great identifying marks of the work of the Spirit in an individual life and to that subject we must now turn.

---

[10]Thomas Watson, *The Ten Commandments*, (Edinburgh: The Banner of Truth Trust, reprinted 1959), pp. 55–56.

6: *The Life of Holiness*

The life of a Christian is one of obedience. His whole being has been reoriented to holiness and to pleasing God. This is one of the major evidences of the regenerating work of the Spirit of God. A servant is one who lives for the will of his master. This is proof that he is a servant and has a servant's heart. Thus the Bible constantly distinguishes the converted from the unconverted in terms of obedience and disobedience. In Romans 8:12–14 Paul writes:

> So then, brethren, we are under obligation, not to the flesh, to live according to the flesh – for if you are living according to the flesh, you must die; but if by the Spirit you are putting to death the deeds of the body, you will live. For all who are being led by the Spirit of God, these are the sons of God.

The sons of God are those who are led by the Holy Spirit. The evidence that they are led of the Spirit is that they live a holy life by the power of the Spirit. That is, they put to death the deeds of the body. Repeatedly Scripture indicates that obedience is the evidence of spiritual life and warns us to examine ourselves in the light of this teaching to make certain that we are in the kingdom (*2 Cor. 13:5; 2 Pet. 1:3–11*).

There is much debate today in evangelical circles in the United States over the meaning of sanctification and its relationship to salvation. In many circles it is taught that it is possible to be a Christian and yet not experience sanctification; that holiness of life is optional and has no ultimate bearing upon one's eternal state. But Scripture's teaching is very clear on this point: without sanctification there is no salvation for without it no one will see the Lord (*Heb. 12:14*). Sanctification (or holiness of life) is simply the direct outgrowth of receiving a new heart and becoming united to Jesus Christ and indwelt by the Holy Spirit. Where the heart has truly become a servant heart then sanctification will be the natural result.

Misunderstanding about sanctification necessarily arises out of a mistaken view of the gospel. When people are taught that all that they need do to be saved is simply to make a decision rather than about the true nature of sin, and are told that repentance is a 'synonym' for faith or that it is not necessary for salvation; when they are taught that submission to the lordship of Christ is unnecessary in entering the kingdom of God and that discipleship is optional; when they are taught that faith does not involve commitment to the person of Christ; when all or any of these things are taught, then the natural result will be a perverting of the biblical teaching on sanctification and its relationship to salvation.

How do we know that in Scripture sanctification is never divorced from justification? By the simple fact that anyone who has been justified is necessarily sanctified. They have received a new heart: whereas the dominant characteristic of life used to be sin it is now holiness. The new life always manifests itself in new obedience. John McArthur rightly stresses how important it is to understand the relation between the gospel and sanctification:

> The church is again facing an age-old problem – the invasion of it by what has become known as 'easy believism' or 'cheap grace' . . . People are told just to 'believe in Jesus' and everything will be settled forever . . . Our Lord recognized the potential problem of an easy believism, as indicated in John 8:30, 31, 'As He spoke these things, many came to believe in Him. Jesus therefore

was saying to those Jews who had believed in Him, "If you abide in My word, then you are truly disciples of Mine."' Jesus affirms that easy believism is inadequate. The concept of easy believism is contrary also to the message of the New Testament epistles regarding salvation and assurance. The life of a true believer is never portrayed as a soft, do-as-you-please existence. The believer is called to a life of obedience, in which faith is verified by conduct. A life of obedience should flow from a Christian's basic relationship to Christ.[1]

LAW AND GRACE

But the question may be asked: 'Does not the Word of God teach that the Christian is no longer under the law, that he is set free from the law of God? And does that not mean that our obedience or sanctification is unrelated to our justification?' This of course raises the whole question of the relationship between law and grace in the life of the Christian. What does Scripture teach us about this relationship?

We have seen that the life of Jesus, as God's servant, was one of perfect obedience to the law of God. Jesus kept God's commandments in every respect, and it is his active obedience and his death on the cross which are the foundation for our redemption and acceptance with God. Jesus has fulfilled the law of God for us. His righteousness, lived out under the law, is what we receive by faith when we come to him. This alone makes us acceptable to God (*Phil. 3:9*). Our obedience contributes nothing to that acceptance. We are justified through the obedience of Another: 'For as through the one man's disobedience the many were made sinners, even so through the obedience of the One the many will be made righteous' (*Rom. 5:19*).

[1]John MacArthur, Jr., *Kingdom Living Here and Now*, (Chicago: Moody, 1980), pp. 5–8.

Thus, when a person becomes a Christian he is united to Christ and delivered from the law. As Paul says, 'You are not under law, but under grace' (*Rom. 6:14*); 'You also were made to die to the Law through the body of Christ . . . We have been released from the Law' (*Rom. 7:4, 6*).

But to understand what Scripture means by this we must answer some important questions. What does it mean to be under the law, to be freed from the law, and to be under grace? Does being under grace mean that the Christian has nothing more to do with the law?

To be 'under the law' means that one is under the authority of the moral law as a standard of acceptance with God. We are morally accountable as created beings to keep the law of God, and to be accepted by God we must keep it perfectly. Not to do so is to come under the curse of God: 'Now we know that whatever the Law says, it speaks to those who are under the Law, that every mouth may be closed, and all the world may become accountable to God'; 'For as many as are of the works of the Law are under a curse; for it is written, "Cursed is everyone who does not abide by all things written in the book of the law, to perform them"' (*Rom. 3:19; Gal. 3:10*).

The law of God is an objective standard which measures righteousness in my relationships with God and with man. But the function of the law is not to save us but to condemn us in our own eyes by revealing to us our sin, to show us that we have fallen short of God's standard. 'Through the Law comes the knowledge of sin' (*Rom. 3:20*). Having thus shown us our sinfulness, and our inability to make ourselves right with God by trying to keep the law, through the ministry of the Holy Spirit the law then shows us our need of the sufficiency of the work of Christ.

When by the grace of God we see our utter sinfulness and helplessness and our guilt and hopelessness, in the light of the law, and flee to Jesus who kept the law perfectly for us, we receive by faith the gift of his righteousness and are declared to be righteous in God's eyes (*Rom. 5:1; 2 Cor. 5:21*). This means that we are delivered from the law's curse, condemnation and judgment since Jesus has borne that in our place as our substitute: 'Christ redeemed us from the curse of the Law, having become a curse for us'; 'There is therefore now no condemnation for those who are in Christ Jesus' (*Gal. 3:13; Rom. 8:1*). In this sense the Christian is no longer under the law; it has ceased to be the ground of condemnation which it once was. For the believer the law has been fulfilled. It demands perfect obedience, but Jesus has met all its requirements. Those who are in Christ have met the requirements of the law in their substitute. Their forgiveness and acceptance with God is based solely on what he has done and not on any success of their own in attempting to keep the law. Their righteousness has been received by faith. In this sense, the law remains the standard of our acceptance with God, but justification assures us that *we* are regarded as having fully obeyed only *in Christ*. The person who is 'in Christ' is now 'under grace'. He will experience the unmerited favour of God to all eternity. He is viewed as righteous in God's eyes because he is in his Son, robed in his righteousness and washed in his blood.

This does not mean that the Christian at once becomes perfectly righteous in personal experience. Justification is a judicial declaration, based on the imputed righteousness of Christ. But if one is now under grace and no longer under the law, does that mean that one no longer has any relationship with the law of God? Have the commandments of God been set aside and become obsolete? No! The Christian is never above the law and can never be lawless. That would be a total misunderstanding of the doctrine of grace. To be 'under grace' means that a person is no longer under the law as a means of acceptance with God. *But*, as a Christian, he is brought into a whole new relationship with the law. It now becomes the rule of his life to direct him as a servant of God, in doing the will of God, for the commandments remain a revelation of the will of God. To be in a state of acceptance with God not only means that one is justified before him for ever, it also means the possession of a Spirit-empowered life which wants to obey his will. That desire does not arise from any concern to achieve acceptance with God, it is rather the response of love in one who is already reconciled. It is obedience motivated by love which God himself puts within us when he gives us a new heart: 'I will put My laws into their minds, and I will write them upon their hearts' (*Heb. 8:10*). The great desire of every renewed heart is to please God by obeying him. If a person claims to be a Christian and is not characterized by obedience to God's commands as the overall direction of his life, then he has never received God's grace.

That it is impossible to separate holiness of life from justification is seen from certain great truths clearly taught in Scripture. They are: the life of Jesus and the nature of his present work; the provisions of the new covenant; and the teaching of Scripture on the nature of the Christian life. We shall look at each of these in turn.

THE LIFE OF JESUS AND HIS PRESENT WORK

When we discussed the servant heart we saw that Jesus is the supreme example of the Christian life and of how it is to be lived. He shows us that the Christian life is a matter of being an obedient servant of God. His life was characterized by perfect obedience or holiness. At no point in his life did he sin. The Scriptures offer abundant proof of this:

Who committed no sin, nor was any deceit found in His mouth (*1 Pet. 2:22*).
And you know that He appeared in order to take away sins; and in Him there is no sin (*1 Jn. 3:5*).

For it was fitting that we should have such a high priest, holy, innocent, undefiled, separated from sinners and exalted above the heavens (*Heb. 7:26*).

Just as Jesus was righteous, Scripture teaches that the believer will also be righteous. As we saw in chapter one, there is a direct correlation between Christ and the believer. 'Whoever keeps His word, in him the love of God has truly been perfected. By this we know that we are in Him: the one who says he abides in Him ought himself to walk in the same manner as He walked' (*1 Jn. 2:5–6*). How did Jesus walk? He walked in obedience. And if he comes to dwell in us by his Spirit then we will walk as he walked – in obedience. It is this which shows us that we really know God, that we are in Him, and are in a state of grace. This is further reiterated in several other verses from the First Epistle of John:

> If you know that He is righteous, you know that everyone also who practices righteousness is born of Him (*1 Jn. 2:29*).
> Little children, let no one deceive you; the one who practices righteousness is righteous, just as He is righteous (*1 Jn. 3:7*).

This is inescapable, and shows us the folly of supposing that one can be a Christian and yet not lead a holy life. The Christian life is a sanctified life because the life of Jesus was a sanctified life. This is further reinforced in that Christ's objective in coming into the world was that he might sanctify us to God: 'For both He who sanctifies and those who are sanctified are all from one Father; for which reason He is not ashamed to call them brethren' (*Heb. 2:11*). Jesus is specifically called the One who sanctifies, and those whom he saves are called 'those who are sanctified'. This is part of his purpose in redemption. Thus Titus 2:13–14 reads, '[we are] looking for the blessed hope and the appearing of the glory of our great God and Savior, Christ Jesus; who gave Himself for us, that He might redeem us from every lawless deed and purify for Himself a people for His own possession, zealous for good deeds'. This is also seen in Ephesians 5:25-26, 'Husbands, love your wives, just as Christ also loved the church and gave Himself up for her; that He might sanctify her, having cleansed her by the washing of the water with the word.' Martyn Lloyd-Jones comments on these verses:

> Notice that this verse has two main functions. The first is the one I have already mentioned, that it reminds us of what the Lord Jesus Christ is continuing to do for the church. But it has a second object also. It tells us why He did the first thing. 'He gave Himself for it; that (in order that)' – this is His object. Why did Christ die? He died 'in order that He might sanctify and cleanse it with the washing of water by the Word'. That is the teaching we have here concerning the doctrine of sanctification.
>
> The first point which we establish and emphasize is this: Forgiveness and deliverance from condemnation, and from hell, are never an end in and of themselves, and must never be considered to be such. They are but a means to a further end. You cannot stop at forgiveness and justification . . . The first principle is that there is nothing which is so utterly unscriptural as to separate justification and sanctification . . . To stop at justification is not only wrong in thought; it is impossible for this reason, that it is something which Christ does; it is He who does this in us. He gave Himself for the church. Why? That He might sanctify and cleanse the church. He is going to do it. The whole trouble arises from the fact that some persist in regarding sanctification as something we decide to go in for. That is never taught anywhere in the Scriptures . . . Sanctification is not something that you and I determine – 'He gave Himself for it, that (in order that) He might sanctify it and cleanse it with the washing of water by the Word'. The

first principle therefore which we must grasp is that sanctification is primarily and essentially something that the Lord Jesus Christ does to us . . . It is His activity, it is His operation; and having died for you, He will do it.[2]

Holiness of life cannot therefore be optional for the Christian. It will naturally occur in every child of God because he is united to Jesus Christ and indwelt by the Spirit of God, whose purpose it is to sanctify those who are redeemed. If this is not taking place there is no evidence that the Holy Spirit dwells in our lives or that we have been justified.

THE PROVISIONS OF THE NEW COVENANT

A life of obedience is a direct result of experiencing the blessings of the new covenant in Christ. The express provisions of this covenant are as follows:

> Then I will sprinkle clean water on you, and you will be clean; I will cleanse you from all your filthiness and from all your idols. Moreover, I will give you a new heart and put a new spirit within you; and I will remove the heart of stone . . . and give you a heart of flesh. And I will put My Spirit within you and cause you to walk in My statutes, and you will be careful to observe My ordinances (*Ezek. 36:25–27*). 'But this is the covenant which I will make with the house of Israel after those days,' declares the Lord, 'I will put My law within them, and on their heart I will write it; and I will be their God, and they shall be My people. And they shall not teach again, each man his neighbor and each man his brother, saying, "Know the Lord," for they shall all know Me, from the least of them to the greatest of them,' declares the Lord, 'for I will forgive their iniquity, and their sin I will remember no more . . . and I will give

[2]D. Martyn Lloyd-Jones, *Life in the Spirit in Marriage, Home and Work: An Exposition of Ephesians 5:18 to 6:9*, (Edinburgh: The Banner of Truth Trust, 1974), pp. 149–152.

them one heart and one way, that they may fear Me always, for their own good, and for the good of their children after them. And I will make an everlasting covenant with them that I will not turn away from them, to do them good; and I will put the fear of Me in their hearts so that they will not turn away from Me (*Jer. 31:33–34; 32:39–40*).

In this covenant God promises to work graciously in the lives of his people. He promises cleansing from the pollution of sin, complete forgiveness of sins, the gift of a new heart on which is written the law of God, the indwelling of the Holy Spirit, a personal knowledge of God and a life of obedience.

In Hebrews 8:6–13, the author of the Epistle to the Hebrews quotes from these new covenant promises given in Jeremiah and reveals that the Lord Jesus Christ is the mediator of the new covenant: 'But now He has obtained a more excellent ministry, by as much as He is also the mediator of a better covenant, which has been enacted on better promises' (*Heb. 8:6*).

It is important to note that, just as the new convenant brings the promise of forgiveness of sins, a new heart, the indwelling of the Holy Spirit and a personal knowledge of God, so there is also the promise of a life of obedience. The law of God is written on the heart and the Holy Spirit has been given to help us to live in conformity with the will of God: 'I will put My Spirit within you and cause you to walk in My statutes, and you will be careful to observe My ordinances' (*Ezek. 36:27*). Just as surely as the Lord gives regeneration and forgiveness of sins, so he will produce a life of obedience in all those who truly know him. This is the express promise of the new covenant which is fulfilled in Jesus Christ. As John Owen wrote over three centuries ago:

The fruit followeth the nature of the tree; and there is no way to change the nature of the fruit, but by changing the nature of the tree which brings it forth. Now, all amendment of life in reformation is but fruit . . . but the changing of our nature is antecedent hereunto. This is the constant course and tenor of Scripture, to distinguish between the grace of regeneration, which it declares to be an immediate supernatural work of God in us and upon us, and all that obedience, holiness, righteousness, virtue, or whatever is good in us, which is the consequent, product, and effect of it. Yea, God hath declared this expressly in his covenant, Ezek. xxxvi. 25–27; Jer. xxxi. 33, xxxii. 39, 40. The method of God's proceeding with us in his covenant is, that he first washeth and cleanseth our natures, takes away the heart of stone, gives a heart of flesh, writes his law in our hearts, puts his Spirit in us; wherein, as shall be evidenced, the grace of regeneration doth consist. The effect and consequent hereof is, that we shall walk in his statutes, keep his judgments and do them, – that is, reform our lives, and yield all holy obedience unto God.[3]

The direct result of experiencing the blessing of the new covenant is a changed life characterized by obedience to God's Word, all flowing from a renewed heart.

THE NATURE OF THE CHRISTIAN LIFE

To teach that it is possible to experience the grace of God without a radical redirection of life is a perversion of the teaching of grace, for 'grace [reigns] *through righteousness* to eternal life through Jesus Christ our Lord' (*Rom. 5:21*). Similarly, Paul writes to Titus, 'For the grace of God has appeared, bringing salvation to all men, instructing us to deny ungodliness and worldly desires and to live sensibly, right-eously and godly in the present age, looking for the blessed hope and the appearing of the glory of our great God and Savior, Christ Jesus; who gave Himself for us, that He might

[3]*The Works of John Owen*, Volume 3, (Edinburgh: The Banner of Truth Trust, reprinted 1965), p. 223.

redeem us from every lawless deed and purify for Himself a people for His own possession, zealous for good deeds' (*Tit. 2:11–14*).

It is now clear that Scripture teaches that it is impossible to separate sanctification from justification. But Scripture also provides abundant indication that obedience is the evidence of regeneration and the indwelling of the Holy Spirit. Obedience does not secure salvation, but salvation is always manifested in a transformed life of holiness. James 2:14–26 emphasizes the point that faith without the works of a holy life is empty faith, that is, it is not saving faith. True faith is confirmed by righteousness.

According to Scripture, it is possible to claim to know God but, in fact, be lost: 'They profess to know God, but by their deeds they deny Him, being detestable and disobedient, and worthless for any good deed' (*Tit. 1:16*). Note the description Paul gives of this unregenerate person: he is *disobedient*. It is the word he uses to describe himself in his lost condition: 'For we also once were foolish ourselves, disobedient, deceived, enslaved to various lusts and pleasures, spending our life in malice and envy, hateful, hating one another' (*Tit. 3:3*). Similarly in Ephesians 2:1–2 lost men are described in the phrase 'sons of disobedience': 'And you were dead in your trespasses and sins, in which you formerly walked according to the course of this world, according to the prince of the power of the air, of the spirit that is now working in the sons of disobedience' (*cf. Eph. 5:6*).

Disobedience characterizes unregenerate, lost men. Obedience characterizes the life of a saved man: he is a 'slave of righteousness' (*Rom. 6:18*). This is why 'No one who is born of God practices sin, because His seed abides in him; and he cannot sin, because he is born of God' (*1 Jn. 3:9*). Where there used to be slavery to sin there is now slavery to righteousness or obedience: 'But thanks be to God that though you were slaves of sin, you became obedient from the heart to that form of teaching to which you were committed, and having been freed from sin, you became slaves of righteousness' (*Rom. 6:17–18*).

The grace of God thus not only brings the forgiveness of sins through the death of Christ, but it also produces a life characterized by obedience as the fruit of regeneration, union with Christ and the indwelling Spirit. God, by his grace, brings us into a completely new relationship with himself. We are now able to obey him and please him by keeping his commandments. Thus, when we say that a man is no longer 'under the law' of God, we do not mean that he no longer has anything to do with the law, but simply that his relationship to the law has been changed. Through the power of the Holy Spirit, the Christian is now able to fulfil the requirements of the law in loving obedience to God: 'For what the Law could not do, weak as it was through the flesh, God did: sending His own Son in the likeness of sinful flesh and as an offering for sin, He condemned sin in the flesh, in order that the requirement of the Law might be fulfilled in us, who do not walk according to the flesh, but according to the Spirit' (*Rom. 8:3–4*). These words are an unambiguous assertion that a justified life is a sanctified life; the evidence of forgiveness is obedience to the commandments of God. The conclusion is inescapable: where there is no progressive sanctification or holiness there is no new life from God and therefore no eternal life.

Precisely this same truth is evident from the description the Word of God gives of the Christian as one who loves God. When the Holy Spirit gives us a new heart he fills that heart with love for God: '. . . the love of God has been poured out within our hearts through the Holy Spirit who was given to us' (*Rom. 5:5*). This is one of the marks of a true Christian. Indeed, Jonathan Edwards says it is the foundation of every other grace in the Christian life. The importance of this love and the fact that it is a distinguishing characteristic of an individual indwelt by the Holy Spirit is seen from the following verses:

> And though you have not seen Him, you love Him (*1 Pet. 1:8*).
> Blessed is a man who perseveres under trial; for once he has been approved, he will receive the crown of life, which the Lord has promised to those who love Him (*Jas. 1:12*).
> If anyone does not love the Lord, let him be accursed (*1 Cor. 16:22*).
> Jesus said to them, 'If God were your Father, you would love Me' (*Jn. 8:42*).

If a man does not love God he is not a Christian. But how is love for God demonstrated in our lives? It is easy *to say* that we love God. But the Scriptures provide us with an infallible test which brings us back once again to the commandments of God. Here, says Scripture, is the proof of our love for God as well as the proof that we have come to know him. The following Scriptures are conclusive:

> And by this we know that we have come to know Him, if we keep His commandments. The one who says, 'I have come to know Him,' and does not keep His commandments, is a liar, and the truth is not in him; but whoever keeps His word, in him the love of God has truly been perfected. By this we know that we are in Him: the one who says he abides in Him ought himself to walk in the same manner as He walked (*1 Jn. 2:3–6*).
> He who has My commandments and keeps them, he it is who loves Me; and he who loves Me shall be loved by My Father, and I will love him, and will disclose Myself to him (*Jn. 14:21*).
> For this is the love of God, that we keep His commandments; and His commandments are not burdensome (*1 Jn. 5:3*).

Circumcision is nothing, and uncircumcision is nothing, but what matters is the keeping of the commandments of God (*1 Cor. 7:19*).

A. W. Pink had described the relationship between love and obedience in this way:

> Said the Lord Jesus, 'He that hath my commandments, and keepeth them, he it is that loveth me' (John 14:21). Not in the Old Testament, the Gospels or the Epistles does God own anyone as a lover of Him save the one who keeps His commandments. Love is something more than sentiment or emotion; it is a principle of action, and it expresses itself in something more than honeyed expressions, namely, by deeds which please the object loved. 'For this is the love of God, that we keep his commandments' (1 John. 5:3).[4]

Obedience to the commandments is not opposed to the biblical emphasis on grace: rather it is the proof that a work of grace has in fact taken place in the heart. A life of holiness is part of the witness of the Spirit to redeemed sinners that we are indeed children of God and are being led by the Spirit. The Christian is a servant whose deepest desire is to know and do the will of God out of love for his Lord. Obedience, therefore, is the natural expression of a new nature, like that of the Lord, to whom every believer has been united. Without this there is no salvation.

[4]A. W. Pink, *Profiting from the Word*, (Edinburgh: The Banner of Truth Trust, 1970), pp. 74–75.

7: *The Practice of Holiness*

Obedience has very practical applications in the life of the servant of God. That is true, first of all, with respect to the Scriptures.

The new heart of a child of God manifests itself in a deep desire to study, know and obey the Word of God. This should seem self-evident; the servant's greatest desire is to know and do the will of his master, as it is revealed in the Word of God. This was demonstrated decisively by the Lord Jesus during his ministry on earth. He shows us the place the Word of God is to have in the life of the servant of God.

In the temptations in the wilderness Jesus revealed the centrality of the Word of God in his own life and the importance of knowing it intimately if one is to walk in obedience before God. In his first response to the devil, Jesus leaves no room for doubt that he has submitted his life to the authority of the Bible. He quotes from Deuteronomy 8:3: 'It is written, "Man shall not live on bread alone, but on every word that proceeds out of the mouth of God" (*Mt. 4:4*).' To heed and obey the Bible is to heed and obey the God of heaven and earth, and Jesus never deviated from that obedience. As he dealt with Pharisees, scribes and Sadducees, he appealed to the Word of God as the authoritative standard for life and truth. He frequently quoted specific passages from memory. He summed up his attitude to God's Word like this: 'I know

Him . . . and keep His word' (*Jn. 8:55*). He had come down from heaven not to do his own will but the will of the Father who had sent him (*Jn. 6:38*). He did that will by obeying the Word of God.

As we have seen, part of the blessing of the new covenant is that we receive a new heart on which is written the law of God; we are given a new life, the primary desire of which is to please God and lovingly to obey him. Consequently, the Christian has a new desire to read, study, memorize, meditate on and obey the Word of God. Why is this so? Because the Holy Spirit uses God's Word to transform our lives. Jesus prayed for the sanctification of his followers through the Word of God: 'Sanctify them in the truth; Thy word is truth' (*Jn. 17:17*). The psalmist expresses the same idea when he says to God, 'How can a young man keep his way pure? By keeping it according to Thy word . . . Thy word I have treasured in my heart, that I may not sin against Thee' (*Ps. 119:9, 11*). Christians are told to 'long for the pure milk of the word, that by it you may grow in respect to salvation' (*1 Pet. 2:2*).

These passages, and the example of the Lord Jesus show us the priority which the Word of God has for the true servant of God. The servant redeems the time to study and memorize God's Word, to hide it in his heart, that he might know and obey his Saviour. If we have the opportunity, but give little time to the Word of God, if there is no real desire to read and study it, if there is no real desire to submit to its authority, then we simply demonstrate that we are not living as servants of God. When Jesus takes residence in the heart of an individual by his Spirit, will he not give him the same desires he had for the Word of God and obedience to it? It is very important that we study theology and doctrine so that we are able rightly to divide the word of truth. But it is even more important that we obey the Word of God. It is practical godliness coupled with theological knowledge that God wants. Our goal should not be knowledge as an end in itself, but Christ-likeness, which is submission to the Word of God in practical obedience and holiness.

PRAYER

A true servant of God will always be a man or woman of prayer. The servant of God lives to know and do the will of God. God has ordained that his will be brought to pass partially through prayer. His servants' lives will therefore be characterized by prayer. And by prayer we mean worship, communion with God and intercession, that is, prayer for others, for God's kingdom and our own needs.

How clearly we see the principle of prayer illustrated in the life of Jesus Christ! He was pre-eminently a man of prayer: 'But He Himself would often slip away to the wilderness and pray' (*Lk. 5:16*). 'And it was at this time that He went off to the mountain to pray, and He spent the whole night in prayer to God' (*Lk. 6:12*). 'And in the early morning, while it was still dark, He arose and went out and departed to a lonely place, and was praying there' (*Mk. 1:35*).

Prayer was a major priority in the life of Jesus. It was not something he engaged in on an occasional basis when it was convenient; he was absolutely committed to it. We learn from him that prayer is not an option in the Christian life. Consequently the entire New Testament urges us to lives of prayer: 'Pray without ceasing . . . The end of all things is at hand; therefore, be of sound judgment and sober spirit for the purpose of prayer . . . Devote yourselves to prayer, keeping alert in it with an attitude of thanksgiving . . . My house shall be called a house of prayer' (*1 Thess. 5:17; 1 Pet. 4:7; Col. 4:2; Lk. 19:46*).

Prayer for the servant of God is not only an activity, it is a way of life. It is that to which he is to be *devoted*, which he is to view as the major *purpose* of his life as a Christian, and which is to be his *constant* practice. As breathing is to physical life, so prayer is to spiritual life. All too often prayer takes a secondary priority to many other commitments but the Word of God emphasizes that prayer is to be our *first* priority. Just as is true of worship, so it is easy to allow prayer to be displaced by other important activities such as preaching, study, teaching, ministry or just plain busyness. But prayer must never be seen as an option. It is not something we do when we feel like it or when it is convenient. It is a matter of commitment and obedience to our Lord. For he has promised that through prayer his will is going to be accomplished and his glory made manifest on the earth.

THE GREAT COMMISSION

When we looked in detail at Jesus' words about the necessity for Christians to deny themselves and take up a cross to follow him, we noted that the context of his words was Peter's taking him aside to rebuke him for saying that he would be crucified by the religious leaders. At that time Jesus rebuked Peter by saying that he was not setting his mind on God's interests but on man's. We saw that one of the major underlying issues in an individual's coming into the kingdom is the surrender of the life to Jesus as Lord with the commitment no longer to live for the interests of self. Jesus amplified this statement when he said: 'For whoever wishes to save his life shall lose it; but whoever loses his life for My sake and the gospel's shall save it' (*Mk. 8:35*). Losing one's life for Jesus' sake and the gospel addresses the whole issue of living for God's interests. God's great concern is the salvation of lost men and women. A true servant will be concerned about the things that concern his master.

Jesus revealed this to be one of the primary motivations of his own heart after his meeting with the woman at the well, described in John 4. His disciples had returned from the town, having purchased food; they requested him to eat something also. But Jesus replied, 'I have food to eat that you do not know about'. They did not understand him, so he went on to explain: 'My food is to do the will of Him who sent Me, and to accomplish His work. Do you not say, "There are yet four months, and then comes the harvest"? Behold, I say to you, lift up your eyes, and look on the fields, that they are white for harvest' (*Jn. 4:34–35*). The food that sustained him was not physical food, but doing the will of God and accomplishing his work. And he equated the will of God and the accomplishing of his work with the ingathering of the harvest, that is, with the gospel and its proclamation. Then he exhorted his disciples to lift up their eyes from the earth and from being absorbed with their own physical needs, to see the vastness of the spiritual harvest, and to be committed to bringing that harvest into the kingdom. Much later, Jesus' final command before returning to his Father expressed the same concern for the evangelization of the world (*Mt. 28:18–20*).

To become a Christian is to commit oneself to God as his servant, and that involves the commitment to further his gospel in this world through the use of our time and money, by means of our personal witness, commitment to world missions and support for missionaries and by our prayers. This is another important aspect of our obedience to our Lord. The purpose of Christ's coming into the world was to seek and save the lost (*Lk. 19:10*). His purpose has not changed, and when he comes into an individual's life, he will manifest the same desire and purpose. A Christian will live for the kingdom of God. He will fulfil the command of Jesus in the Sermon on the Mount, 'But seek first His kingdom and His righteousness; and all these things shall be added to you' (*Mt. 6:33*). The seeking of the kingdom of God is to be foremost in our living and praying as the Lord's prayer makes plain.

As God's servant, the Christian is supremely interested in God being glorified on the earth. This takes place when his kingdom comes into the hearts of men through Jesus Christ in response to the gospel. Jesus himself prayed and taught his followers to pray for labourers to be sent forth into the harvest field (*Mt. 9:38*). God's heart beats with compassion for a lost and dying world, and his desire, expressed in the life of Christ, is to bring men and women to the truth of his gospel. As God's servants, next to our relationship with the Lord himself, a concern for his kingdom should be uppermost in our minds. We have been redeemed not to promote our own ambitions but to serve our Lord by seeking first his kingdom and his righteousness:

> Christ's command means that we should be devoting all our resources of ingenuity and enterprise to the task of making the gospel known in every possible way to every possible person . . . The truth about salvation has been made known to us, not for us simply to preserve (though we must certainly do that), but also, and primarily, for us to spread. The light is not meant to be hidden under the bushel. It is meant to shine; and it is our business to see that it shines. 'Ye are the light of the world . . .' says our Lord. He who does not devote himself to evangelism in every way that he can is not, therefore, playing the part of a good and faithful servant of Jesus Christ.[1]

Given the serious implications of the gospel, we need to ask ourselves some heart-searching questions. Are our lives marked by the practice of obedience to the Word of God? Are we men and women of true holiness who love the Lord with all our hearts and prove it by keeping his commandments? Do we have a hunger and love for the Word of God? Are our lives characterized by prayer? Do we seek first the kingdom

[1] J. I. Packer, *Evangelism and the Sovereignty of God*, pp. 33–34.

THE CHRISTIAN

of God and his righteousness? It is not enough to have a profession of Christianity. If the Holy Spirit truly dwells within us he will manifest his presence in changed lives. Are we really a new creation?

J. C. Ryle writes:

It requires far more than most people seem to think necessary, to save a soul. We may be baptized in the name of Christ, and boast confidently of our ecclesiastical privileges; we may possess head knowledge, and be quite satisfied with our own state; we may even be preachers, and teachers of others, and do 'many wonderful works' in connection with our Church: but all this time are we practically doing the will of our Father in heaven? Do we truly repent, truly believe on Christ, and live holy and humble lives? If not, in spite of all our privileges and profession, we shall miss heaven at last, and be for ever cast away. We shall hear those awful words, 'I never knew you: depart from Me.'

The day of judgment will reveal strange things. The hopes of many, who were thought great Christians while they lived, will be utterly confounded. The rottenness of their religion will be exposed and put to shame before the whole world. It will then be proved that to be saved means something more than 'making a profession.' We must make a 'practice' of our Christianity as well as a 'profession.' Let us often think of that great day: let us often 'judge ourselves, that we be not judged,' and condemned by the Lord. Whatever else we are, let us aim at being real, true, and sincere.[2]

[2]J. C. Ryle, *Expository Thoughts on the Gospels: Matthew*, (Edinburgh: The Banner of Truth Trust, reprinted 1986), p.70.

8: *Communion with God*

The most precious reality in Christian experience following the regenerating work of the Holy Spirit is personal knowledge of God. This is a promise of the new covenant and it becomes ours through Jesus Christ: 'And this is eternal life, that they may know Thee, the only true God, and Jesus Christ whom Thou hast sent' (*Jn. 17:3*). The word 'know' here means much more than the knowledge of facts – to know *about*. It expresses the knowledge of intimacy in personal relationship. (Scripture describes the intimacy of physical union within marriage as 'knowing' e.g. in Matthew 1:24–25: 'Then Joseph being raised from sleep did as the angel of the Lord had bidden him, and took unto him his wife: and *knew* her not till she had brought forth her first-born son: and he called his name Jesus' (KJV).)

In redemption God takes those who have been alienated and separated from him and who have no knowledge of him, and brings them into a personal, experiential relationship with himself. Knowing facts about God does not guarantee that a person really knows him, although Christian doctrine is *meant* to bring us to an experiential knowledge of God. Martyn Lloyd-Jones comments:

> It is possible for us to develop a false notion of knowledge . . . to take a purely theoretical and academic interest in truth and knowledge, to make knowledge an end in and of itself – the purely theoretical and academic approach . . . To vary the expression, this danger is one of knowing 'about' a subject rather than knowing it.

'Knowing about'! What a vital distinction this is. What a difference there is between preaching about the gospel and preaching the gospel! It is possible to preach round the gospel and say things about it without ever presenting it. That is quite useless – indeed it can be very dangerous. It may be true of us that we know 'about' these things, but do not really know them. And this, of course, becomes all-important when we realize that the whole end and object of theology is to know God! A Person! Not a collection of abstract truths, nor a number of philosophical proposi-tions, but God! A Person! To know Him! – 'the only true God, and Jesus Christ, whom thou hast sent!'[1]

Those who are born again of the Spirit of God experience the presence of God. A sure evidence of the work of the Spirit is to know God as our Father. There is a filial spirit produced in the heart of a child of God, 'For you have not received a spirit of slavery leading to fear again, but you have received a spirit of adoption as sons by which we cry out, "Abba! Father!" The Spirit Himself bears witness with our spirit that we are children of God . . . And because you are sons, God has sent forth the Spirit of His Son into our hearts, crying, "Abba! Father!"' (*Rom. 8:15–16; Gal.4:6*). This involves intimacy, communion, fellowship, tenderness and endearment. Many Scripture passages indicate that the Christian has fellowship with the Father and with the Lord Jesus: 'What we have seen and heard we proclaim to you also, that you also may have fellowship with us; and indeed our fellowship is with the Father, and with His Son Jesus Christ' (*1 Jn. 1:3*).

Communion and fellowship with God is the privilege and right of every child of God and is to some degree the experience of each one. The following verses express God's desire that all believers should enjoy it:

[1]D. Martyn Lloyd-Jones, *The Puritans: Their Origins and Successors*, (Edinburgh: The Banner of Truth Trust, 1987), pp. 28, 30, 31–32.

Since therefore, brethren, we have confidence to enter the holy place by the blood of Jesus, by a new and living way which He inaugurated for us through the veil, that is, His flesh, and since we have a great priest over the house of God, let us draw near with a sincere heart in full assurance of faith, having our hearts sprinkled clean from an evil conscience and our bodies washed with pure water (*Heb. 10:19–22*).

God is faithful, through whom you were called into fellowship with His Son, Jesus Christ our Lord (*1 Cor. 1:9*).

Behold, I stand at the door and knock; if anyone hears My voice and opens the door, I will come in to him, and will dine with him, and he with Me (*Rev. 3 :20*).

If anyone loves Me, he will keep My word; and My Father will love him, and We will come to him, and make Our abode with him (*Jn. 14:23*).

The eternal God is a dwelling place, and underneath are the everlasting arms (*Deut. 33:27*).

Through the work of Christ and because of our union with him, Christians enjoy access to God: 'But now in Christ Jesus you who formerly were far off have been brought near by the blood of Christ . . . in whom we have boldness and confident access through faith in Him' (*Eph. 2:13; 3:12*). God desires communion with his people. He wants them to experience his love. He has done everything necessary through the work of the Lord Jesus and the ongoing work of the Holy Spirit to make that experience a reality. Consequently our 'hope does not disappoint, because the love of God has been poured out within our hearts through the Holy Spirit who was given to us' (*Rom. 5:5*). Thus the child of God experiences communion, fellowship and intimacy with God – an experience of the love of God! Once again John Owen finely comments:

I come now to declare what it is wherein peculiarly and eminently the saints have communion with the Father;

[91]

and this is LOVE, – free, undeserved, and eternal love. This the Father peculiarly fixes upon the saints; this they are immediately to eye in him, to receive of him, and to make such returns thereof as he is delighted withal. This is the great *discovery* of the gospel: for whereas the Father, as the fountain of the Deity, is not known any other way but as full of wrath, anger, and indignation against sin, nor can the sons of men have any other thoughts of him (*Rom. i. 18; Isa. xxxiii. 13, 14; Hab. i. 13; Ps. v. 4–6; Eph ii. 3*), – here he is now revealed peculiarly as love, as full of it unto us; the manifestation whereof is the peculiar work of the gospel, Tit. iii. 14.[2]

As Owen says, this is the great discovery of the gospel. When a person is brought to know God through Jesus Christ, he finds that the love of God is the love of a Father. What a wonderful truth! It totally transforms life. Every child of God is personally embraced by his love and has been brought into an experience in which love which passes knowledge will be experienced forever. The believer has a foretaste here of the world of love which is heaven and it transforms his priorities in this present life:

Spiritual realities are of the highest import in the kingdom of God. What are these spiritual delights which must be sought first? . . . First in importance is *communion with God* . . . have we discovered that our souls have basic needs which tangible things will never satisfy? Have we learned by a felt experience that 'Man shall not live by bread alone, but by every word . . . of God' (Matt. 4:4)?

Made in the image of God, man's deepest longings can only be met in communion with the Lord most high. Human souls can make contact with a spiritual world which has no sensual appeal. Yet the soul has feelings of its own. Our world has finely honed the physical senses and despised spiritual experience. There are very real delights

[2]*The Works of John Owen*, Volume 2, p. 19.

which some never know because they only trade in the material. Have you known God and his glorious presence in holy embraces of personal fellowship? . . . How can anyone, whose soul has been in the presence of his Maker, suggest that there is more important business for a creature than to know and adore the Lord of glory? . . . There are glorious riches to be had in the kingdom of God, spiritual riches, the foremost of which is knowing the only true God.[3]

THE OBJECTIVE TRUTH OF THE LOVE OF GOD

When we say that God is love we are speaking about one of the foundational truths of the Christian life. We are talking about the very essence of the heart of God and his attitude towards each of his children as individuals. The apostle John writes, 'We have come to know and have believed the love which God has for us' (*1 Jn. 4:16*), and adds, 'We love, because He first loved us' (*1 Jn. 4:19*). The Bible tells us that before one can love God, he must first of all come to know and then believe the love which God has for him. Before we can experience the love of God, we must first of all respond to the revelation of his love. This is the basis of communion with God: the fact of his love. Communion with God is based upon objective revelation of the love of God which he has made manifest in Christ. This is why, over and over again, the Word of God sets before us the objective fact of the love of God demonstrated in the work of Christ:

We know love by this, that He laid down His life for us . . . (*1 Jn. 3:16*).
By this the love of God was manifested in us, that God has sent His only begotten Son into the world so that we might live through Him. In this is love, not that we loved God,

---

[3]Walter J. Chantry, *God's Righteous Kingdom*, (Edinburgh: The Banner of Truth Trust, 1980), pp. 22–23, 25.

but that He loved us and sent His Son to be the propitiation for our sins (*1 Jn. 4:9–10*).

But God demonstrates His own love toward us, in that while we were yet sinners, Christ died for us (*Rom. 5:8*).

For God so loved the world, that He gave His only begotten Son, that whoever believes in Him should not perish, but have eternal life (*Jn. 3:16*).

Here we have the proof of the love of God. It is revealed in the person and work of the Lord Jesus. And the truly transforming thing about understanding the love of God for us, is the realization that God loves *me*, as an individual. He desires *me* for himself. He desires *my* fellowship, for the Saviour died for *me* personally, and I am very dear to him. This is what draws my heart out to seek communion with him, as I respond to his love by faith.

To know the love of God in this way is a wonderful experience indeed but it can be hindered. For the devil will oppose the Christian's apprehending the truth of the love of God, and will seek to interpose unbelief, resulting in our withdrawing from the Lord rather than a joyous abandonment to him. It should be understood that all that we have been talking about in previous chapters is necessary for an individual to experience communion with God. There must be total submission of the life to live for the glory of God in worship and obedience. Thus the Christian is called upon to enter into intimate communion with God. But the devil will seek to do all he can to hinder this experience. John Owen voiced a concern in his day that many were subject to such a hindering work:

Many dark and disturbing thoughts are apt to arise in this thing. Few can carry up their hearts and minds to this height by faith, as to rest their souls in the love of the Father; they live below it, in the troublesome region of hopes and fears, storms and clouds. All here is serene and quiet. But how to attain to this pitch they know not. This is the will of God, that he may always be eyed as benign, kind, tender, loving, and unchangeable therein; and that peculiarly as the Father, as the great fountain and spring of all gracious communications and fruits of love. This is that which Christ came to reveal, – God as a Father, John i. 18; that name which he declares to those who are given him out of the world, John xvii. 6. And this is that which he effectually leads us to by himself, as he is the only way of going to God as a Father, John xiv. 5, 6; that is, as love: and by doing so, gives us the rest which he promiseth; for the love of the Father is the only rest of the soul.[4]

Believing the love of God, and responding to it in faith, is the only way to enter into communion with God and find rest in him. Apart from this one will experience insecurity and uncertainty. But God wants his children to dwell with him in an open, face to face relationship of love – a life ideally of unbroken communion and fellowship. To that end faith must understand and rest constantly on the work of the Lord Jesus. He came to reveal the true nature of God to us. He came to bring us into a wholly new relationship with the Father, into the conscious experience of his fatherly love, his favour, his protection and his care. God is a Father! He is love! And as a Father, he has a deep desire that his children will know his love and become secure in it. His heart is one that is full of warmth, compassion, tenderness and love. Surely one of the great truths that we find in the parable of the prodigal son is the father heart of God. There we see yearning, aching love that desired a lost rebellious son to return. And when he did return in true repentance he found not a stern judge, but a father who dearly loved him and showered him with affection. In such words Christ reveals the intense desire of God himself.

Love has desire at the centre of its being. Why did God send his Son, and give him as a propitiation for sin? Why did he forgive us, justify us and adopt us into his family? Because he

[4]*The Works of John Owen*, Volume 2, p. 23.

desires us for himself. He loves us with stupendous love. He loves us to the point of passion, and desires fellowship and intimate communion with his children. Just as in the Song of Solomon the bride rejoices in the realization of the love of her bridegroom, so we can rejoice in Christ's love for his church and say, 'I am my beloved's, and his desire is for me' (*Song 7:10*).

God's passionate desire shines throughout the life of the Lord Jesus who came to seek and to save the lost (*Lk. 19:10*). Our God is a seeking God because his heart is a heart of love. All the statements that he makes in his Word about his people confirm this fact. He speaks to us in words of intense affection and joy and longing. All his thoughts of us began with love: 'In love He predestined us to adoption as sons through Jesus Christ to Himself' (*Eph. 1:4–5*). Love is the great reason for his purpose in redemption and adoption. He must bring us to himself.

Again and again we are told that those who are truly called of God and are his children are greatly *beloved* by him: 'knowing, brethren *beloved* by God, His choice of you' (*1 Thess. 1:4*); 'among whom you also are the called of Jesus Christ; to all who are *beloved* of God in Rome' (*Rom. 1:6–7*). If you are a Christian you are *greatly beloved* by God your Father! To be 'beloved' means to be 'greatly loved, to be 'dear to the heart'. This is exactly the same word the Father used of Jesus at his baptism: 'This is My *beloved* Son, in whom I am *well-pleased*' (*Mt. 3:17*). His attitude towards his children is the same as his attitude towards the Lord Jesus! This is expressed even more forcefully in John 17:22–23, where Jesus in his high priestly prayer says, 'And the glory which Thou hast given Me I have given to them; that they may be one, just as We are one; I in them, and Thou in Me, that they may be perfected in unity, that the world may know that Thou didst send Me, *and didst love them, even as Thou didst love Me.*' What an incredible truth – the Father loves those he has redeemed with the same love with which he loves his very own Son! This is echoed throughout Scripture:

> The Lord your God is in your midst, a victorious warrior. He will exult over you with joy, He will [renew you] in His love, He will rejoice over you with shouts of joy (*Zeph. 3:17*).
> As the bridegroom rejoices over the bride, so your God will rejoice over you (*Is. 62:5*).
> I am the Lord your God, the Holy One of Israel, your Savior . . . you are precious in My sight, you are honored and I love you (*Is. 43:3–4*).
> I have loved you with an everlasting love; therefore I have drawn you with lovingkindness (*Jer. 31:3*).
> But God, being rich in mercy, because of His great love with which He loved us (*Eph. 2:4*).

This is the heart of our God and Father. He rejoices over his children with shouts of joy and singing as a bridegroom rejoices over his bride. We are precious in his sight, we are honoured and the delight of his heart.

> If we are 'accepted in the Beloved,' then, first, our persons are accepted: we ourselves are well-pleasing to him. God looks upon us now with pleasure. Once he said of men that it repented him that he had made them, but now when he looks at his people he never repents that he made us . . . he takes delight in us. Look at your own children; sometimes they grieve you, but still you are pleased with them; it is a pleasure to have them near you; and if they are long out of your sight you grow anxious about them . . . Our Father is truly pleased with us: our very persons are accepted of God. He delights in us individually; he thinks of us with joy, and when we are near to him it gives pleasure to his great heart.[5]

[5]C. H. Spurgeon, *The Metropolitan Tabernacle Pulpit*, Volume 29, (Edinburgh: The Banner of Truth Trust, reprinted 1971), p. 403.

THE CHRISTIAN

RESPONSE TO THE LOVE OF GOD

On the basis that God is love and has demonstrated his love towards us in the giving of the Lord Jesus, we now have the wonderful privilege as his children of responding to the manifestation of that love. There ought to be before us the glorious expectation of continuous fellowship with him. It is not enough that we know the facts related to the love of God as our Father, it is necessary that we *respond* to his love if we would experience communion with him.

> Our communion . . . with God consisteth in his *communication of himself unto us, with our returnal unto him* of that which he requireth and accepteth, flowing from that *union* which in Jesus Christ we have with him.[6]

There are three major aspects to the response we are called to make to the revelation of the love of God if we are to hold communion and fellowship with him.

First of all we must respond with obedient, holy lives. One cannot walk in sin and walk in fellowship with the Holy One of Israel: 'Can two walk together, except they be agreed?' (*Amos 3:3*, KJV); 'If we say that we have fellowship with Him and yet walk in darkness, we lie and do not practice the truth' (*1 Jn. 1:6*). These Scriptures, as well as many others, show us that the Lord has intimate communion with those whose hearts and lives are pure before him. Psalm 25:14 reinforces this when it says, 'The secret [intimacy] of the Lord is for those who fear Him.' 1 Peter 1:14-17 equates the fear of God (an attitude which includes love) with an obedient life (*cf. Prov. 8:13*). In John 14:21 and 15:10 Jesus promises the manifestation of himself and the experience of his love to the one who obeys his commandments. Obedience or holiness of life and

[6]*The Works of John Owen*, Volume 2, p. 8-9.

communion with God are directly related to one another. Only a child can commune with the Father but all God's children are also his servants.

A second essential aspect of our response to the revelation of the love of God is faith. We must believe what our Father has revealed to us about his heart-attitude towards us, receive it and respond to it in love. It is very important that we spend time in meditation on the Scriptures which speak of the love of God lest we become guilty of unbelief through an unbalanced concept of God. Because of our innate sinfulness we naturally tend to think of God as being angry, unapproachable and disapproving. It is true that the Lord disapproves of sin and if we are walking in known sin we will experience his displeasure. But where there is an earnest endeavour to walk in the light in submission and holiness and obedience before our God, then we can respond to his love and have boldness of access unto him through the Lord Jesus Christ. We must beware of harbouring hard thoughts about God, of refusing to believe what he has revealed of himself and of keeping him at a distance. The great desire of God's heart is that we believe in his love, receive it and thus experience deep intimacy and communion with him.

John Owen points out that in order to experience true communion with God, we have to fight an aggressive fight of faith against the suggestions of Satan. Otherwise these truths will not be believed and received into our hearts:

> It is exceeding *acceptable* unto God, even our Father, that we should thus hold communion with him in his love, – that he may be received into our souls as one full of love, tenderness, and kindness, towards us. Flesh and blood is apt to have very hard thoughts of him, – to think he is always angry, yea, implacable . . . Now, there is not anything more grievous to the Lord nor more subservient to the design of Satan upon the soul, than such thoughts as these . . . it is exceeding grievous to the Spirit of God to be so

slandered in the hearts of those whom he dearly loves . . .
The Lord takes nothing worse at the hands of his, than such
hard thoughts of him, knowing full well what fruit this
bitter root is like to bear, what alienations of heart, – what
drawings back, – what unbelief . . . in our walking with
him . . .

Communion consists in *giving* and *receiving*. Until the
love of the Father is received, we have no communion with
him therein. How, then, is the love of the Father to be
received, so as to hold fellowship with him? The answer, By
faith. The receiving of it is the believing of it . . .

Let . . . the soul frequently eye the love of the Father
. . . So *eye* it as to *receive* it. Unless this be added, all is in vain
as to any communion with God. We do not hold com-
munion with him in any thing until it is received by faith.
This, then, is what I would provoke the saints of God unto,
even to believe this love of God for themselves and their own
part, – believe that such is the heart of the Father towards
them, – accept of his witness herein. His love is not ours in
the sweetness of it until it be so received. Continually, then,
act thoughts of faith on God, as love to thee, – as embracing
thee with the eternal free love before described. When the
Lord is, by his word, presented as such unto thee, let thy
mind know it, and assent that it is so; and thy will embrace
it, in its being so; and all thy affections be filled with it. Set
thy whole heart to it; let it be bound with the cords of this
love.[7]

There is nothing so transforming to a human soul as to come to
know the love which God has for it. But as the apostle John
writes in 1 John 4:16, these truths must be believed. The
proper response to the revelation of the love of God is faith.

But then there is a third aspect to the response which flows
out of faith and which completes the cycle of giving and
receiving in our communion with God; it is the response of
love itself. The natural response of a redeemed sinner to

[7]*The Works of John Owen*, Volume 2, pp. 34–35, 22, 34.

God's love is to love him in return. 'We love, because He first loved us' (*1 Jn. 4:19*).

This means that just as we are his beloved so he is to be our beloved. He is to be beloved by us! He must ever be preeminent in our affections. He is to be our first love, our life, the total joy and satisfaction of our hearts, our all in all. Just as our Lord delights in his own and rejoices over them with singing and gladness of heart, so they are to delight in him and sing to him with gladness and thanksgiving: 'Delight yourself in the Lord; and He will give you the desires of your heart . . . O come, let us sing for joy to the Lord; let us shout joyfully to the rock of our salvation' (*Pss. 37:4; 95:1*). He is to be the rest of their souls, the one who meets the deep longings of their heart. Many Scriptures remind us that God has made us for himself and that in the heart of every redeemed saint is a hunger and thirst to know God intimately. He is to be to us the bread of life and the fountain of living waters:

> Whom have I in heaven but Thee? And besides Thee, I desire nothing on earth. My flesh and my heart may fail, but God is the strength of my heart and my portion forever (*Ps. 73:25–26*).
> O God, Thou art my God; I shall seek Thee earnestly; my soul thirsts for Thee, my flesh yearns for Thee, in a dry and weary land where there is no water . . . Because Thy lovingkindness is better than life, my lips will praise Thee. So I will bless Thee as long as I live; I will lift up my hands in Thy name. My soul is satisfied as with marrow and fatness, and my mouth offers praises with joyful lips . . . For Thou hast been my help, and in the shadow of Thy wings I sing for joy (*Ps. 63:1, 3–4, 7*).
> As the deer pants for the water brooks, so my soul pants for Thee, O God. My soul thirsts for God, for the living God (*Ps. 42:1–2*).
> Like an apple tree among the trees of the forest, so is my beloved among the young men. In his shade I took great delight and sat down, and his fruit was sweet to my taste. He

has brought me to his banquet hall, and his banner over me
is love (*Song 2:3–4*).
But whatever things were gain to me, those things I have
counted as loss for the sake of Christ . . . that I may know
Him' (*Phil. 3:7, 10*).

These verses make it abundantly clear that when a man is
redeemed he receives a new heart in which God himself
becomes the central desire and love. George Burrowes makes
this point in his commentary on the Song of Solomon:

The desire which in the heart of the saint absorbs every
other, is for the manifestation of the love of the Lord Jesus,
through the influences of the Holy Spirit; and this love is
thus ardently desired, because its effect is more reviving
and exhilarating than any of the pleasures of sense, even
wine, the most refreshing of them all.

This desire is not a blind instinct or a fanatical impulse,
but springs from an intelligent apprehension of the
excellency of the nature of Christ, as transcending every
thing known to man, more than the holy anointing oil of
the sanctuary surpassed any other perfume; – an excel-
lence so rich, that the pure in heart, and they only, love
him, and they cannot do otherwise than love him.

The thought of the excellency of the character of Christ
and of the influences of the Holy Spirit shedding abroad
his love in the heart, creates the desire of coming as near to
him as possible, without any delay – of running to him;
and as our own insufficiency and weakness are felt sensibly
at such times, we pray for the attracting power of his grace
and for the strength of his Spirit. This desire is never
expressed in vain; with kingly majesty and condescension,
he brings us into confidential communion with him apart
from the world; this communion is attended with fulness
of joy and a holy exultation in his superior grace . . .

At such times, in near communion with Jesus, and with
the affections in vigorous exercise, we feel our Lord
amazingly precious . . . Jesus towers on high in majesty

and grandeur; the citron-tree is his emblem, and illustrates his character as combining majesty with beauty, as affording shelter and protection to his people, as capable of satisfying the wants of the soul . . . Hence, when we come under the shadow of Christ, we have great delight, and find food for the hungering heart; his ways are ways of pleasantness and all his paths are peace.[8]

Love for God does not consist only in the love of obedience and reverence. It also consists in the giving of the heart to him in response to the declaration of his love. It means that we seek to see him as the chief delight, satisfaction and joy of our heart; that we prize his fellowship as more to be desired than any other experience on earth. He must have the central place in the affections. We were made for God and he alone is the true rest of our souls. No other human relationship, indeed nothing in this world can satisfy our hearts. And the call of the gospel is for men to abandon the pursuit of trying to find life in this world, to turn to God and, through Christ, to enter into his love. Thus we learn to love God supremely and to have him first in the heart so that he becomes our very life. The command of Scripture, that we love the Lord our God with *all* our heart, soul, mind and strength, is both our highest duty and privilege. This is why the Lord Jesus says, 'He who loves father or mother more than Me is not worthy of Me; and he who loves son or daughter more than Me is not worthy of Me' (*Mt. 10:37*).

In Revelation chapter 2, the exalted Christ addresses the Ephesian church and commends them for their labour, their doctrinal purity and their zeal. But he rebukes them for the fact that they have lost their first love. They were doing many right things, but they had failed to maintain close fellowship with their Lord. He had been displaced from the place of

[8]George Burrowes, *A Commentary on the Song of Solomon*, (Edinburgh: The Banner of Truth Trust, reprinted 1973), pp. 105–106, 109, 111.

pre-eminence in their affections. These believers are warned that, if they do not repent, he will remove their candlestick. In other words, he will remove their testimony. They may continue to be busy, they may even have great knowledge of the Word of God, but there will be no light and no joy.

A first-love relationship which is maintained through worship and communion is obviously of the highest priority to Jesus Christ. Communion with him is not something that can be incidental. It is primary to our calling as Christians and to our ministry. We need to remember the words of Jesus spoken to Martha to which we have already referred: only one thing is needful. *Christ* must come first in every area of our lives. He must be our life, our chief joy and the ultimate satisfaction of our hearts. We must be careful to watch over our hearts, lest anything else be allowed to displace him from that first place in our affections. We must set aside the necessary time on a consistent basis to be alone with him in prayer. Communion with him is our highest calling.

This whole concept runs counter to much modern-day Christianity which majors on activities and programmes and say very little about cultivating intimacy with Jesus Christ and the Father through worship and communion. But Christ's word to the Ephesian church should be a sobering word to the excessively busy evangelical church of our day which has lost true biblical priorities.

There is another reason, too, why the experiential reality of perceiving God is unfamiliar country today. The pace and preoccupations of urbanized, mechanized, collectivized, secularized modern life are such that any sort of inner life (apart from the existentialist *Angst* of society's misfits and the casualties of the rat race) is very hard to maintain. To make prayer your life priority, as countless Christians of former days did outside as well as inside the monastery, is stupendously difficult in a world that runs you off your feet and will not let you slow down. And if you attempt it, you will certainly seem eccentric to your peers, for nowadays involvement in a stream of programmed activities is decidedly 'in,' and the older ideal of a quiet, contemplative life is just as decidedly 'out.' That there is widespread hunger today for more intimacy, warmth, and affection in our fellowship with God is clear from the current renewal of interest in the experiential writings of the Puritans and the contemplative tradition of prayer as expounded by men like Thomas Merton. But the concept of Christian life as sanctified rush and bustle still dominates, and as a result the experiential side of Christian holiness remains very much a closed book.[9]

Hebrews 10:19–22 explains that, on the basis of the work of Christ, the Christian has been given boldness of access into the holy place, that is, the place of God's abiding presence. We are exhorted to draw near to that place with a pure heart, in sincerity of faith. But to draw near means much more than simply coming aside from time to time to seek God. It means drawing near with a whole heart in faith, so that we dwell continually in God's presence in unbroken communion and fellowship.

'Draw near' is a term that suggests not only a confident, diligent seeking, but also great love and tenderness. Since all Christians have been brought near to God by the blood of Christ (*Eph. 2:13*), they are exhorted to draw near to the Father (*Heb. 10:22*). All the work necessary to give us access to the Father has been accomplished, all the barriers have been removed. It is now our responsibility as Christians to respond to God's initiative by drawing near to him.

The first biblical occurrence of the term 'draw near' is in Genesis 48:10 in an incident where Jacob blesses Joseph's sons. There we are told that Joseph brought them near to his father, who embraced them and kissed them. Jacob showered

[9] J. I Packer, *Keep in Step with the Spirit*, (Old Tappan: Revell, 1984), pp. 74–75.

them with love and tender affection. When the Septuagint (the Greek translation of the Hebrew Old Testament) was produced, the same Greek word was used in Genesis 48:10 as is found in Hebrews 10:22, 'draw near with a sincere heart in full assurance of faith'. That picture of Joseph's sons being brought so near to their grandfather that he could touch them beautifully portrays our fellowship with God.

When we draw near to God, we are assured that he draws near to us (*Jas. 4:8*), and we are in turn drawn into his embraces of love and affection, for we are his children and his beloved ones. If we will but respond in faith and love to the overtures of our Lord, get alone with him, seek his face and maintain our first-love relationship with him, fellowship with him will be increasingly prized. We will experience his love and he will truly satisfy our heart. It cannot be said too often that God desires our love and fellowship and that we experience his love, not because he needs anything from his creatures but purely and simply because he is love. He loves all his children. In the words of one writer:

> *God loves to be longed for, He loves to be sought,*
> *For He sought us Himself with such longing and love:*
> *He died for desire of us, marvellous thought!*
> *And He longs for us now to be with Him above.*

Close fellowship with the living God is the calling and privilege of every Christian. In regeneration the Holy Spirit produces a filial spirit in the heart of every child of God so that his natural heart cry is 'Abba, Father!' He has come to know God. Christians are beloved of him, and he of them, and their deepest desire is to commune with him in love. This is their right, purchased at the high cost of the blood of Jesus.

'My Beloved,' – this is a sweet name which our love takes liberty to apply to the Lord Jesus. His inexpressible beauty has won our affection, and we cannot help loving him . . . We are carried away by the torrent of his goodness, and have no longer the control of our affections. As long as we live we must and will love the altogether lovely One. Yes, he is, and must be to me, 'My Beloved.'

But suppose, – suppose for a moment that we loved and had no right to love . . . The beloved was longed for, but could not be grasped . . . Thank God, this is not the case with the soul enamoured of Christ Jesus; for he freely presents himself in the gospel as the object of our confidence and love. Though he be infinitely above us, yet he delights to be one with all his loving ones, and of his own will he gives himself to us. A polluted sinner may love the perfect Saviour, for there is no word in Scripture to forbid . . .

Suppose yet once again that, though we loved, and rightly loved, and actually possessed the beloved object, yet our affection was not returned. Ah, misery! to love and not be loved! Blessed be God, we can not only sing, 'My Beloved is Mine,' but also, 'I am his.' He values me, he delights in me, he loves me! . . . The truth that Jesus calls me his is enough to make a man dance and sing all the way between here and heaven. Realize the fact that we are dear to the heart of our incarnate God, and amid the sands of this wilderness, a fountain of overflowing joy is open before us.[10]

[10]C. H. Spurgeon, *The Metropolitan Tabernacle Pulpit*, Volume 27, (Edinburgh: The Banner of Truth Trust, reprinted 1971), pp. 698–700.

9: *The Life of Faith*

The presence of the Holy Spirit in our lives always gives rise to a life of faith. In fact, from beginning to end the Christian life is a life of faith. Without it there is no true Christianity. Faith is necessarily a distinguishing mark of the life of the Spirit for it is his gift as well as being exercised by the individual. Where the Holy Spirit is resident, faith will be born. This is of major importance in the Word of God; that it is indispensable to the Christian life may be seen from the following Scriptures:

> Therefore having been justified by faith, we have peace with God through our Lord Jesus Christ (*Rom. 5:1*).
> And without faith it is impossible to please Him, for he who comes to God must believe that He is, and that He is a rewarder of those who seek Him (*Heb. 11:6*).
> But My righteous one shall live by faith; and if he shrinks back, My soul has no pleasure in him (*Heb. 10:38*).
> For we walk by faith, not by sight (*2 Cor. 5:7*).
> I have been crucified with Christ; and it is no longer I who live, but Christ lives in me; and the life which I now live in the flesh I live by faith in the Son of God, who loved me, and delivered Himself up for me (*Gal. 2:20*).
> But the righteous man shall live by faith (*Rom. 1:17*).

But what is faith? At first glance it may seem to be a relatively easy thing to define: it is simply believing God. But on closer examination of the biblical descriptions of faith, we find that definition is inadequate. Believing God is obviously involved and is an important element of faith. But it can be a purely intellectual activity, going no further than the mind. Biblical faith is much more than intellectual assent to God's truth, as James makes clear when he defines the nature of saving faith. (*Jas.2:14–26*). He makes the point that faith is not only a matter of profession and mental assent to certain truths, for, he says, the demons believe and shudder. He states that there is such a thing as 'dead' faith as well as 'living' faith, and the major distinction between the two is the element of commitment. True biblical faith affects the whole man in his mind, will and emotions and is evidenced by a life committed to Christ. It does involve the intellect, since there are certain truths which must be believed; but biblical faith must also involve commitment, or it will be no different from the faith of demons.

In Colossians 2:6 Paul writes, 'As you therefore have received Christ Jesus the Lord, so walk in Him.' How does an individual receive Christ? The Scriptures teach that he is received by faith. A proper understanding of how one receives Christ by faith will therefore define how we are to live the Christian life.

In bringing us to salvation, the Spirit of God reveals the guilt of our sin and shows us our total inability to save ourselves or make ourselves right with God through our own efforts. Then, through the Word of God in the gospel, he reveals the all-sufficiency of Christ as Lord and Saviour. And the result is that, by the grace of God, the sinner turns to Christ in faith to receive salvation. What, then, are the essential elements of saving faith?

First of all the sinner is brought to the conviction that the message of God's Word is truth: 'And for this reason we also constantly thank God that when you received from us the word of God's message, you accepted it not as the word of men, but for what it really is, the word of God, which also performs its work in you who believe' (*1 Thess. 2:13*). Faith's foundation is the Word of God. Faith's object is the God of the Word.

The sinner is thus brought to the point of believing God's Word and the essential truths that it reveals about God and Christ, about sin and the way of salvation. He understands that Jesus Christ is Lord and God and the only mediator between God and man. He understands that Christ's work on the cross in the shedding of his blood in substitutionary atonement, providing an imputed righteousness for all who believe on him, is the only means of forgiveness and salvation. The Spirit of God reveals to him that his own works are unacceptable to God and cannot bring him salvation. These are all important truths. They are essential aspects of faith, yet they are not all there is to true biblical faith. We cannot define faith solely in terms of objective truths. A person can 'believe' all the right things about God and Christ and salvation and, as we have seen, still be lost, for saving faith also involves several other factors.

As the Spirit of God reveals these truths to a lost sinner he also sets before him the person of Christ as the object of faith. Faith in him means trusting *in* the Lord Jesus Christ, which means coming to Christ in personal repentance, commitment and dependence.

Furthermore, biblical faith is always accompanied by repentance. There must be a turning *from* sin as well as a turning *to* Christ as Lord and Saviour, and a cessation of all attempts to rely upon our own attempts at self-righteousness to qualify us for acceptance with God. We turn from all works, be they religious, social or moral, and commit ourselves to Jesus Christ alone as Saviour, depending upon him and trusting him to save. In such a conversion we cannot continue to live a life in sin opposed to God. In repentance we have turned from the world, from our sins and from self-rule and committed ourselves to Jesus as Lord. We know the commitment of heart which, as we have seen from Mark 8, belongs to every true disciple of Christ.

The object of saving faith, then, is always the person
of Christ, the foundation of faith is the Word of God, and
the exercise of faith involves the elements of commitment,
trust and dependence. J. I. Packer makes these comments
about the nature of saving faith in his Foreword to John
MacArthur's book *The Gospel According to Jesus*:

> God has joined faith and repentance as the two facets of
> response to the Savior and made it clear that turning to
> Christ means turning from sin and letting ungodliness go.
> Biblical teaching on faith joins credence, commitment,
> and communion; it exhibits Christian believing as not only
> knowing facts about Christ, but also coming to him in
> personal trust to worship, love, and serve him . . . Simple
> assent to the gospel, divorced from a transforming com-
> mitment to the living Christ, is by biblical standards less
> than faith, and less than saving, and to elicit only assent of
> this kind would be to secure only false conversions.[1]

And John MacArthur himself says:

> The gospel Jesus proclaimed was a call to discipleship, a
> call to follow Him in submissive obedience, not just a plea
> to make a decision or pray a prayer. Jesus' message
> liberated people from the bondage of their sin while it
> confronted and condemned hypocrisy. It was an offer of
> eternal life and forgiveness for repentant sinners, but at
> the same time it was a rebuke to outwardly religious people
> whose lives were devoid of true righteousness. It put
> sinners on notice that they must turn from sin and embrace
> God's righteousness. It was in every sense good news, yet
> it was anything but easy-believism . . . One segment of
> evangelicalism has even begun to propound the doctrine
> that conversion to Christ involves 'no spiritual commit-
> ment whatsoever.' Those who hold this view of the gospel
> teach that Scripture promises salvation to anyone who
> simply believes the facts about Christ and claims eternal

[1]John MacArthur, Jr., *The Gospel According to Jesus*, (Grand Rapids:
Zondervan, 1988), p. ix.

THE CHRISTIAN

life. There need be no turning from sin, no resulting change in life-style, no commitment – not even a *willingness* to yield to Christ's lordship. Those things, they say, amount to human works, which corrupt grace and have nothing to do with faith. The fallout of such thinking is a deficient doctrine of salvation. It is justification without sanctification, and its impact on the church has been catastrophic. The community of professing believers is populated with people who have bought into a system that encourages shallow and ineffectual faith. Many sincerely believe they are saved but are utterly barren of any verifying fruit in their lives.[2]

If true saving faith involves knowledge, commitment, trust and dependence so does the Christian's life of faith. Conversion is but the beginning of a believing life. As A. W. Pink says, 'The Christian life is the habitual continuance of what took place at conversion, the carrying out of the vows then made, the putting of it into practice.'[3]

Let us look at each of these elements of faith and how they relate to the living of the Christian life.

COMMITMENT

The fact that faith as a way of life involves commitment is seen from the description Scripture gives of the life of Christ. Hebrews 3:2 says, 'He was faithful to Him who appointed Him.' One of the leading characteristics of Christ's life was faithfulness to God. Faith always involves faithfulness and a commitment to God to serve him, walk with him and love him. Those who come to Christ by faith become like him, in that they become men and women whose lives are characterized by commitment to live for God. As James puts it, their faith will be evidenced by their works. God, his will

---

[2]John MacArthur, Jr., *The Gospel According to Jesus*, pp. 21–22.
[3]A. W. Pink, *An Exposition of Hebrews*, (Grand Rapids: Baker, 1954), p. 729.

and the things of eternity will be first in the life as opposed to the interests of self and the things of this world.

This is also seen in the example of Abraham who is called the father of the faithful. Abraham is a pattern of the life of faith, and the descriptions that are given of his life in Hebrews 11 teach us a great deal about the nature of biblical faith:

> By faith Abraham, when he was called, obeyed by going out to a place which he was to receive for an inheritance; and he went out, not knowing where he was going. By faith he lived as an alien in the land of promise, as in a foreign land, dwelling in tents with Isaac and Jacob, fellow heirs of the same promise; for he was looking for the city which has foundations, whose architect and builder is God (*Heb. 11:8–10*).

When Abraham was called by God, he obeyed. He believed God and his response to God's revelation of himself to him was obedience, that is, commitment. He went forth depending on God to guide him, provide for him and protect him. He trusted God to fulfil his word to him. Bound up with this trust and dependence was Abraham's life of commitment. Apart from commitment – a life of surrender and obedience – it is useless to talk about trust and dependence.

Abraham was called to leave his country, his culture and his kindred and to commit himself to follow God. He had to leave the companionship of people devoted to this world, and, in so committing themselves to God, he and the other patriarchs like him became aliens, strangers, foreigners, pilgrims and exiles. They lived in tents in the land of promise as followers and worshippers of God. They did not live for this world but for eternity, looking not for an earthly city but for a heavenly one. By faith they committed themselves to God, and the whole focus of their lives was changed. Their perspective became that of the world to come and their hope was in

God himself. Scripture assures us that all who are born again of the Holy Spirit follow in their footsteps. That which characterized the life of Abraham and the other pioneers of faith will also characterize the life of every child of God.

The man of faith, the man with a regenerate heart, has a renewed mind and a new perspective. He sees life differently from the natural man, from the perspective of the future. His life is one of faith; he is living for eternity and no longer for this world. Scripture is emphatic in its teaching that a true Christian does not live for the world or the things which dominate the world, for he has died to it and his heart has been given to God:

> Do not love the world, nor the things in the world. If anyone loves the world, the love of the Father is not in him. For all that is in the world, the lust of the flesh and the lust of the eyes and the boastful pride of life, is not from the Father, but is from the world. And the world is passing away, and also its lusts; but the one who does the will of God abides forever (*1 Jn. 2:15–17*).

> You adulteresses, do you not know that friendship with the world is hostility toward God? Therefore whoever wishes to be a friend of the world makes himself an enemy of God (*Jas 4:4*).

> But may it never be that I should boast, except in the cross of our Lord Jesus Christ, through which the world has been crucified to me, and I to the world (*Gal. 6:14*).

The kingdom of God and eternity, not the kingdom of this world, dominate the heart of a true Christian. The believer has a completely different perspective and focus because he has experienced the renewing power of the Holy Spirit; there is permanent evidence in his life of true faith. It is a life committed to God and his purposes.

We may further see the relationship between commitment and faith and appreciate the importance of a biblical perspective, from the testimony of Paul in the Second Epistle to the Corinthians:

But in everything commending ourselves as servants of God, in much endurance, in afflictions, in hardships, in distresses, in beatings, in imprisonments, in tumults, in labor, in sleeplessness, in hunger, in purity, in knowledge, in patience, in kindness, in the Holy Spirit, in genuine love, in the word of truth, in the power of God; by the weapons of righteousness for the right hand and the left, by glory and dishonor, by evil report and good report; regarded as deceivers and yet true; as unknown yet well-known, as dying yet behold, we live; as punished yet not put to death, as sorrowful yet always rejoicing, as poor yet making many rich, as having nothing yet possessing all things (*2 Cor. 6:4–10*).

Therefore we do not lose heart, but though our outer man is decaying, yet our inner man is being renewed day by day. For momentary, light affliction is producing for us an eternal weight of glory far beyond all comparison, while we look not at the things which are seen, but at the things which are not seen; for the things which are seen are temporal, but the things which are not seen are eternal (*2 Cor. 4:16–18*).

Paul begins by saying that he is a servant of God and then he lists the difficulties, trials and hardships confronting him. But it is obvious he is committed to be faithful in the face of it all. No matter what comes against him, he will do the will of God. He may experience sorrow and even depression (*2 Cor. 7:5–6*), but this does not affect his commitment to obey God for he has an eternal perspective. He realizes that all he is going through will one day issue in eternal glory. He looks, he says, not on things that are seen, which are temporal, but on things not seen, which are eternal. This is faith. It sees beyond this world to an eternal kingdom. And, for God's sake, the believer will thus live and endure.

This is reiterated in Hebrews 12:1–2:

Therefore, since we have so great a cloud of witnesses surrounding us, let us also lay aside every encumbrance,

and the sin which so easily entangles us, and let us run with
endurance the race that is set before us, fixing our eyes on
Jesus, the author and perfecter of faith.

The race the writer had in mind here is clearly the race of
faith. The believer is involved in a long-distance endurance
race. Because of the persecution, hardship and testing the
Hebrew Christians were faced with the temptation to turn
aside. The author writes to encourage them along the path of
faith – the path of endurance and commitment. In the face of
harsh experience he calls them to set aside a sin which can
easily trip them up – unbelief.

We have already seen that the life of faith is a life of
commitment to a person. It is commitment to holiness and
endurance, a commitment to live for God's will above
everything else in this world. Scripture abounds in encouragement to help us to do this: 'Blessed is a man who
perseveres under trial; for once he has been approved, he will
receive the crown of life, which the Lord has promised to
those who love Him' (*Jas. 1:12*); 'In this you greatly
rejoice, even though now for a little while, if necessary, you
have been distressed by various trials, that the proof of your
faith, being more precious than gold which is perishable,
even though tested by fire, may be found to result in praise
and glory and honor at the revelation of Jesus Christ' (*1 Pet.
1:6-7*).

These verses tell us that trials are given to test our
profession of faith. They try our commitment to see if we will
endure, for Scripture says that only those who persevere
under trials will receive the crown of life. Therefore only
those who manifest a life of commitment have true biblical
faith. The New Testament constantly brings us back to the
fact that faith is evidenced in a life of commitment to Jesus
Christ, a commitment which *remains* through suffering, trial
and difficulty. Faith submits to the circumstances of God's

choosing; it endures and trusts him in the midst of all adversities.

The man of faith sees present circumstances from an eternal perspective. He lives looking to God, believing him, trusting him and depending upon him. And therefore his response to circumstances is completely different from that of men of the world. There are certain things a child of God believes about God's character; he trusts in his promises and depends upon him for strength and wisdom to do his will. The Christian is like Moses who, by faith, left Egypt and 'endured, as seeing Him who is unseen' (*Heb. 11:27*). Faith sees God and endures; its focus is the person of God. No one can walk a life of faith in commitment and endurance who does not trust God and depend upon him. These all go hand in hand.

TRUSTING GOD

The life of faith is conditioned by the Word of God. It frames our perspective on all of life. What the Word of God teaches about the character and being of God controls our thinking and is foundational to the whole life of faith. Hence Paul's exhortation in Romans 12:2: 'And do not be conformed to this world, but be transformed by the renewing of your mind, that you may prove what the will of God is, that which is good and acceptable and perfect.' The Holy Spirit uses the Word of God to renew the mind of the believer and to transform his life so that he fulfils the will of God.

There are certain fundamental truths about God on which faith must depend at all times. The Scriptures teach that God is sovereign and in control of all circumstances (*Ps. 104:19; Dan. 2:20–21; Eph. 1:11*); that he is good and can do nothing wrong (*Pss. 25:8; 86:5*); that he is holy and perfect in all his ways and dealings with man (*Deut. 32:3–4*); that he is love and is vitally concerned for his children (*1 Pet. 5:7;*

1 Jn. 4:8); that he is all-wise and can never make a mistake (*Is. 40:13–14; Dan. 2:20–21*); that he is truthful and can never lie (*Num. 23:19*); that he is faithful and always true to his word – he cannot fail (*Josh. 1:5–9; Ps. 90:4*); that he is omnipotent and able to bring his will to pass in every circumstance (*Is. 40:25–26; Jer. 32:17*); that he is present with his people to undertake for them in every circumstance (*Josh. 1:5, 9; Is. 41:10; Mt. 28:20*).

The Christian believes these facts about God and responds to circumstances in the light of them. An example of this is recorded in Psalm 22, which is a prophetic psalm about the suffering the Messiah would face on the cross:

> My God, my God, why hast Thou forsaken me? Far from my deliverance are the words of my groaning. O my God, I cry by day, but Thou dost not answer; and by night, but I have no rest. Yet Thou art holy, O Thou who art enthroned upon the praises of Israel. In Thee our fathers trusted; they trusted, and Thou didst deliver them. To Thee they cried out, and were delivered; in Thee they trusted, and were not disappointed (*Ps. 22:1–5*).

In the midst of his sufferings and trials, when it seemed that God had utterly forsaken him, Jesus looked to the character of God, his holiness and faithfulness. He *trusted* in him.

God is faithful to his promises and is able to fulfil them both for his Son and for all those who are his servants. He promises Christians that he will never leave them or forsake them; he will empower them, guide them, protect them, provide for them and accomplish his purposes through them. The believer trusts God to do what he said he would do, even though that may appear to be impossible. In both life and ministry, the Christian is called upon to trust the God 'who gives life to the dead and calls into being that which does not exist' (*Rom. 4:17*). Abraham is again an example of faith here.

He believed God's word and trusted him to do what, from a human perspective, was totally impossible:

> In hope against hope he believed, in order that he might become a father of many nations, according to that which had been spoken, 'So shall your descendants be.' And without becoming weak in faith he contemplated his own body, now as good as dead since he was about a hundred years old, and the deadness of Sarah's womb; yet, with respect to the promise of God, he did not waver in unbelief, but grew strong in faith, giving glory to God, and being fully assured that what He had promised, He was able also to perform (*Rom. 4:18–21*).

Abraham was faced with a situation that seemed to contradict everything he had come to believe about God. God had made a promise to him about an heir, but now he and Sarah were beyond the point of being able to be parents. Yet God kept assuring him that he would be the father of many nations. Abraham took a long hard look at his circumstances but he did not waver in unbelief. He looked to God and his ability, convinced that he was able to do what he had promised even though that appeared to be impossible. He responded to his circumstances in faith, allowing God's word and character rather than his own circumstances to condition his perspective and response.

> Abraham did not give way to weakness, he did not stagger, but rather was 'made strong' – made strong, either in faith, or else made strong by faith. I believe that both are true. He was made strong in his faith, but also he was made strong by his faith . . . Abraham, instead of looking only at the difficulties in terms of his own body and the age of Sarah, instead of staggering at the greatness of the promise, Abraham, instead of stumbling at those two things, looked to God and looked at God. That is the real secret of faith. The main explanation of the troubles and difficulties which most of us experience in our lives is that,

instead of keeping our eyes steadfastly on God, we look at ourselves and our weaknesses and the staggering greatness of the life to which we have been called. We look at these things and we become weak and begin to stagger. Abraham did not stagger for the reason that he gave glory to God. He kept his eyes on God, and he looked to God.[4]

Abraham was strong because he knew God, he knew his promise and he believed what God had told him and trusted him to bring it to pass. In the walk of faith, the Christian believer must do exactly what Abraham did. There are many promises given in the Word of God which speak of his faithfulness to provide, to guide, to give wisdom, to protect, to strengthen and to empower for ministry. We are expected to know these promises and to trust the Lord to fulfil them in our lives.

The same can be said about facing difficult and trying circumstances. We must respond to them in faith by trusting God and not doubting him. The Word of God tells us that he has a purpose for all he allows into our life, and it is ultimately for our good and his glory: 'And we know that God causes all things to work together for good to those who love God, to those who are called according to His purpose' (*Rom. 8:28*). God is never arbitrary. Beyond our understanding, he has many purposes in the circumstances he sovereignly permits to occur in our lives. He uses trials and difficulties to prune us and develop our character, to test our faith and to build it, to keep us humble and dependent, to chasten us for sin, to develop in us an intimate knowledge of himself and, above all, to prepare us for eternity.

Given these perspectives we are called upon to exercise faith by responding to circumstances with submission, trust, rejoicing, thanksgiving and praise (*Jas. 1:2–4; Rom. 5:3–5*).

---

[4]D. Martyn Lloyd-Jones, *Romans: An Exposition of Chapters 3:20–4:25: Atonement and Justification*, (Edinburgh: The Banner of Truth Trust, 1970), pp. 220–221.

This is the evidence that we are really walking by faith. We are called upon to trust God and not to doubt him. Fear, doubt, anxiety, discouragement, self-pity, disappointment, bitterness and anger are all emotions that must be resisted if we are to walk by faith and glorify God. The servant of God cannot be passive in this life of faith for it is an intense warfare. There must be an aggressive resistance, by the grace of God, to all that is contrary to his will and Word, and an aggressive obedience to all that is consistent with them. Paul exhorts Timothy to 'fight the good fight of faith'. The life of faith is a life of warfare with the world, the flesh and the devil. The man of faith is a soldier who endures for the sake of Christ, and, while not yet perfect, lives a life characterized by victory. He is an overcomer as Jesus promised he would be. As J. C. Ryle says:

> The true believer is not only a soldier, but a *victorious* soldier. – He not only professes to fight on Christ's side against sin, the world, and the devil, but he does actually fight and *overcome*.
>
> Now this is one grand distinguishing mark of true Christians. Other men, perhaps, like to be numbered in the ranks of Christ's army. Other men may have lazy wishes, and languid desires after the crown of glory. But it is the true Christian alone who does the work of a soldier. He alone fairly meets the enemies of his soul – really fights with them, and in that fight overcomes them . . . if you would prove you are born again and going to heaven, you must be a victorious soldier of Christ. If you would make it clear that you have any title to Christ's precious promises, you must fight the good fight in Christ's cause, and in that fight you must conquer.
>
> *Victory* is the only satisfactory evidence that you have a saving religion . . . You respect the Bible, and read it occasionally. You say your prayers night and morning. You have family prayers, and give to Religious Societies. I thank God for this . . . But how goes the battle? How does

the great conflict go on all this time? Are you overcoming the love of the world and the fear of man? Are you overcoming the passions, tempers, and lusts of your own heart? Are you resisting the devil and making him flee from you? How is it in this matter? You must either rule or serve sin, and the devil, and the world. There is no middle course. You must either conquer or be lost . . . You must fight the good fight of faith, and endure hardships, if you would lay hold of eternal life. You must make up your mind to a daily struggle, if you would reach heaven. There may be short roads to heaven invented by man; but ancient Christianity, the good old way, is the way of the cross – the way of conflict. Sin, the world, and the devil must be actually mortified, resisted, and overcome.[5]

The conflict of faith involves a temptation to accept the negative emotions of fear and anxiety and doubt in our relationship with God. But we must firmly resist every tendency to give in to the thoughts and emotions which fuel these feelings and attitudes. We must allow our minds to be renewed by the Word of God and in the light of his character and promises begin to thank him and praise him for who he is and for his faithfulness. We will then be strengthened to trust God, and will be set free from a negative depressed frame of mind. We must learn to believe his promises and all that Scripture tells us about his sovereignty, his goodness, his love and faithfulness. We must refuse to allow ourselves to fall into these negative emotions. To give in to them is sin for they are an evidence of unbelief. Do not fear! Do not be anxious! Rejoice! Trust! Give thanks! These are the commands of the Word of God to us in every circumstance.

Amy Carmichael, who served her Lord faithfully for over fifty years in India and experienced much suffering in her life, writes these words about trials and faith:

But perhaps sometimes in an incomparably lesser trial the

[5]J. C. Ryle, *Holiness* p. 236.

tempter has disturbed us by persuading us to look for an explanation. We find ourselves saying, I wonder why. *Faith never wonders why* . . . 'I am learning never to be disappointed, but to praise,' Arnot of Central Africa wrote in his journal long ago . . . I think it must hurt the tender love of our Father when we press for reasons for His dealings with us, as though He were not love, as though not He but another chose our inheritance for us, and as though what He chose to allow could be less than the very best and dearest that Love Eternal had to give . . . Thereafter, not seeing, not hearing, not feeling, we walk by faith, finding our comfort . . . in the Scriptures of truth: 'I know whom I have believed, and am persuaded that He is able to keep that which I have committed unto Him against that day . . . And we know that all things work together for good to them that love God.' With Him who assures us of this there is no variableness, neither shadow that is cast by turning. His word stands true. In that truth we abide satisfied . . . And so I have come to this: our Lord is sovereign.[6]

DEPENDENCE

The Christian is thus not only one who trusts God; he is also one who lives in dependence upon God for the strength, empowering and enabling to do his will. There is a conscious turning from all self-reliance to live in a state of dependence upon God. This comes from the inner heart-attitude of humility implanted by the Holy Spirit in regeneration. The servant heart is a humble heart.

The Greek word for humility is *tapeinos*. The root idea is to be low-lying, of low degree, to be brought low. It means having an inner heart-attitude of lowliness, a lowly estimate of oneself. It is the opposite of pride which is the attitude of independence and self-sufficiency; it is 'poverty of spirit'.

[6]Amy Carmichael, *Rose from Brier*, (Fort Washington Pa.: Christian Literature Crusade, 1933), pp. 111–113.

The Christian is conscious of his own weakness, inability and inadequacy and this leads to an increasing dependence on the Holy Spirit. Just as we came to realize that we have no ability or strength to please God or to save ourselves and therefore we cast ourselves upon Christ alone for salvation, so we must depend upon God to live the Christian life. The Scriptures consistently teach that believers do not have the innate capacity to live the life to which God has called them. They are thus brought to depend more fully upon the sufficiency, strength and enabling of the Spirit of God:

> Apart from Me you can do nothing (*Jn. 15:5*).
> For if anyone thinks he is something when he is nothing, he deceives himself (*Gal. 6:3*).
> I know, O Lord, that a man's way is not in himself; nor is it in a man who walks to direct his steps (*Jer. 10:23*).
> For I know that nothing good dwells in me, that is, in my flesh (*Rom. 7:18*).
> Not that we are adequate in ourselves to consider anything as coming from ourselves, but our adequacy is from God (*2 Cor. 3:5*).
> And we proclaim Him, admonishing every man and teaching every man with all wisdom, that we may present every man complete in Christ. And for this purpose also I labor, striving according to His power, which mightily works within me (*Col. 1:28–29*).
> I can do all things through Him who strengthens me (*Phil. 4:13*).
> But I say, walk by the Spirit, and you will not carry out the desire of the flesh (*Gal. 5:16*).

J. I. Packer has written:

> There is need for *the most deliberate humility*, self-distrustful and self-suspicious, in all our fellowship with God. Why? Because, whereas God is perfectly holy, pure, good, and unchangeably faithful in performing his promises, we are none of these things . . . We were born sinful

in Adam, and sinful inclinations, dethroned but not yet destroyed, still remain in us now that we are in Christ. We are constantly beset by the seductions, deceptions, and drives of lawless pride and passion, of defiant self-assertion and self-indulgence . . . So we need to get down very low before our Saviour God and to cultivate that sense of emptiness, impotence, and dependence that Jesus called poverty of spirit (Matthew 5:3).[7]

The Christian life, both in practical day to day living as well as in ministry to others, calls for a moment by moment dependence born out of an attitude of lowliness. Too often in modern evangelicalism Christians are unwittingly drawn into a life of subtle self-sufficiency which blunts the effectiveness of their lives and ministries.

One context in which this can occur is where too much emphasis is placed on activities. We begin to equate spirituality primarily with doing certain things. But such activity can very easily displace God from our life so that we begin to depend on the activity rather than the Lord himself. I remember a very earnest Christian confiding in me that he could not understand why, after he had been faithful to spend time alone with the Lord, that fifteen minutes later he could yell at his wife. His problem was that in a subtle way the activity had displaced God and he had begun to depend on his 'quiet time' rather than on the Lord himself. The Christian has to keep constantly on guard against all self-reliance.

Now a Christian should be involved in activities. He *should* have a 'quiet time', memorize scripture, do Bible study, fast and be involved in ministry. But activities do not make a person spiritual. For while a spiritual person *will* be involved in all of those basic activities and more, one can be involved in those activities and still be terribly unspiritual and proud.

[7]J. I. Packer, *Keep in Step with the Spirit*, p. 124.

The same can be said of knowledge. We may think that because we have accrued a certain amount of knowledge, or received a certain kind of training, that we are qualified to minister. There can be a subtle dependence on these things with the result that there is no sense of helplessness and inability. The person feels qualified and sufficient to meet the challenges of ministry and therefore there is no real sense of dependency on the Spirit of God. Now there is nothing wrong with knowledge, degrees or training, but they must never be allowed to produce an attitude of self-sufficiency. The point is, we must constantly be on guard against depending on anything other than the Lord himself in our life and our ministry. We need power for life and ministry and that comes only as we walk in fellowship with God in dependence upon him. All our resources – our knowledge, training, activities, programmes, preaching, teaching, witnessing and zeal – mean absolutely nothing unless the power of the Holy Spirit attends them. 'The king is not saved by a mighty army; a warrior is not delivered by great strength. A horse is a false hope for victory; nor does it deliver anyone by its great strength. Behold, the eye of the Lord is on those who fear Him, on those who hope for His lovingkindness' (*Ps. 33: 16–18*). Psalm 44:1–3 expresses the same spirit: 'O God, we have heard with our ears, our fathers have told us, the work that Thou didst in their days, in the days of old. Thou with Thine own hand didst drive out the nations; then Thou didst plant them; Thou didst afflict the peoples, then Thou didst spread them abroad. For by their own sword they did not possess the land; and their own arm did not save them; but Thy right hand, and Thine arm, and the light of Thy presence, for Thou didst favor them.'

What God is saying is that natural ability alone does not equip an individual to be able to do his will. It is not a matter of having all the right resources – a mighty army, chariots, swords, horses, great physical strength – these are not sufficient. There must be the power of God and that means we are shut up to a life of dependence.

Gardiner Spring recognized this need for dependency in the preaching ministry, but his remarks apply to every area of the Christian life:

> The dependence of men on the efficient power of the Holy Spirit is one of the great peculiarities of the Christian faith . . . Human instrumentality is never so effective in this work as when it is most conscious of its own weakness and keeps itself most out of sight. It is the secret agency of God that accomplishes it; and no flesh may glory in his presence . . . If there be any hope for the anxious heart of a minister of the Gospel, this dependence on the power of the Holy Spirit is the rock on which he rests . . . No matter how learned or simple the instructions of the pulpit may be; no matter how rich and varied, or how well adapted and spiritual; did it speak with the tongue of Paul, or of angels, it would be powerless without the superadded power of God . . . Never, till the excellency of God's power is revealed, is the power of the pulpit known. Nor may we hope that God's mighty arm will be revealed, until this truth is known and felt. One reason why God's Spirit is so often withheld is that this great truth is lost sight of; or, if not lost sight of, is coldly recognized, and does but form a feature of that languid and dead orthodoxy, which, while it may govern the views, has very little to do with the heart. This is not the place which such a truth deserves; it must be thought of, and prized, and leaned upon, and prove itself the most delightful of all incitements to effort . . . The strength of the pulpit is in its own conscious weakness, and in God's almighty power . . . There is power in the pulpit when it is thus allied to the power of God. We can do everything through him, without whom we can do nothing.[8]

[8]Gardiner Spring, *The Power of the Pulpit*, (Edinburgh: The Banner of Truth Trust, reprinted 1986), pp. 76–81.

We were not created to live in self-reliance and self-dependence. We were created to live in a *state* of total dependence upon God. This is why Scripture exhorts believers to be filled with the Spirit (*Eph. 5:18*), to walk in the Spirit (*Gal. 5:16*), to live by faith in the Son of God (*Gal. 2:20*), to look to Jesus (*Heb. 12:2*), to be strong in the Lord and in the strength of his might (*Eph. 6:10*) and to abide in Christ (*Jn. 15:4–5*). To live the Christian life the believer must live in God and have his focus on God.

True dependency means much more than simply coming to God to depend on him when there is a conscious need. It means learning to dwell in God in a habitual state of dependence. Deuteronomy 33:27 refers to God as a 'dwelling place', a 'refuge' as the King James Version translates it. But the word means more than simply a place of protection. It also means an abode, a dwelling place, a habitation. It is used of the temple as the dwelling place of God, for a lair as the dwelling of animals and for a home as the dwelling of men. Thus the eternal God is to be our habitation, our abode, the One in whom we live and who is our very life. Thus Psalm 91:1 says, 'He who dwells in the shelter of the Most High, will abide in the shadow of the Almighty.' Here again the word 'dwell' is used. C. H. Spurgeon says it refers to those who '*habitually reside* in the mysterious presence'. This is what it means to dwell in God; not simply turning to him occasionally when we think we need him, but habitually, unceasingly living in a *state* of dependence upon him.

Other Scriptures communicate the same truth in different words. For example, Deuteronomy 10:20 says, 'You shall fear the Lord your God; you shall serve Him and *cling* to Him, and you shall swear by His name' (*cf. Deut. 11:22; 13:4; 30:20; Josh. 22:5; 23:8*). We are commanded here not only to fear God and serve him, but also to *cling* to him, in loyalty and devotion. The same verb is used in a different context in Genesis 2:24: 'For this cause a man shall leave his father and his mother, and shall *cleave* to his wife; and they shall become one flesh.' Here it denotes a physical and emotional intimacy between a married couple. That is but a reflection of our relationship with God (*Eph. 5:31–32*). Our union with him results in affection, intimacy and dependence. We become *one* with him.

There are several passages of Scripture which use the word 'cleave' or 'cling' in an illustrative way which will help us to visualize what the word means:

> The Lord will make the pestilence *cling* to you until He has consumed you from the land . . . And He will bring back on you all the diseases of Egypt of which you were afraid, and they shall *cling* to you (*Deut. 28:21, 60*).
> Therefore, the leprosy of Naaman shall *cleave* to you and to your descendants forever (*2 Kings 5:27*).
> Who can count the clouds by wisdom, or tip the water jars of the heavens, when the dust hardens into a mass, and the clods *stick together*? (*Job 38:37–38*).
> I will set no worthless thing before my eyes; I hate the work of those who fall away; it shall not *fasten its grip* on me (*Ps. 101:3*).
> May my tongue *cleave* to the roof of my mouth, if I do not remember you (*Ps. 137:6*).
> And in that you saw the iron mixed with common clay, they will combine with one another in the seed of men; but they will not *adhere to one another*, even as iron does not combine with pottery (*Dan. 2:43*).

These Scriptures help us to understand the nature of our relationship with God. We are commanded to dwell in the Lord, to cling to him, to adhere to him like glue, to be one with him and to live in him in a state of unceasing dependence. This will mean a constant turning from self-reliance, from leaning on one's own strength, wisdom, understanding and resources to depend upon God alone. Proverbs 3:5–6 says, 'Trust in the Lord with all your heart, and do not lean on your own understanding. In all your ways acknowledge Him, and He will make your paths straight ' Matthew Henry comments on these verses:

> We must repose an entire confidence in the wisdom, the power, and the goodness, of God, assuring ourselves of the extent of his providence to all the creatures and all their actions. We must therefore *trust in the Lord with all our hearts*; *v.* 5 we must believe that he is able to do what he will, wise to do what is best, and good, according to his promise, to do what is best for us, if we love him and serve him. We must, with an entire submission and satisfaction, depend upon him to perform all things for us, and not *lean to our own understanding*; as if we could, by any forecast of our own, without God, help ourselves, and bring our affairs to a good issue. Those who know themselves, cannot but find their own understanding to be a broken reed, which, if they lean to, it will certainly fail them. In all our conduct we must be diffident of our own judgment, and confident of God's wisdom, power, and goodness, and therefore must follow Providence, and not force it . . .
>
> We must not only in our judgment believe that there is an over-ruling hand of God ordering and disposing of us and all our affairs, but we must solemnly own it, and address ourselves to him accordingly. We must ask his leave, and not design any thing but what we are sure is lawful. We must ask his advice, and beg direction from him, not only when the case is difficult (when we know not what to do, no thanks to us that we have our eyes up to him), but in every case, be it ever so plain. We must ask success of him, as those who know *the race is not to the swift.*[9]

This constant dependence and trust in the Lord results in joy, peace, security and rest. David proved this: 'I have set

[9]Matthew Henry, *A Commentary on the Whole Bible*, Volume 3, p.803.

the Lord continually before me; because He is at my right hand, I will not be shaken' (*Ps. 16:8*). Similarly, Isaiah says: 'Thou wilt keep him in perfect peace, whose mind is stayed on thee: because he trusteth in thee. Trust ye in the Lord for ever: for in the Lord Jehovah is everlasting strength' (*Is. 26:3–4*, KJV). The Lord is to be constantly before us so that no matter what we face, we know that his hand is upon our lives for our good, and we trust him and consciously depend on him for his love, wisdom, strength, guidance, protection, provision and power. In fact, all through the Psalms, David spoke of the Lord as his helper, his trust, his shepherd, his strength, his rock, his refuge, his fortress, his shield, his deliverer, his stronghold, his portion, his joy, his love, his satisfaction, his chief delight, his counsellor, his teacher, his guide, etc. This is what we discover when we walk with the Lord and depend upon him.

For the man of faith the focus of his life is the person of God. He is to trust him implicitly, just as a little child in all his helplessness and weakness trusts in his father. Whether it is in living as a Christian, or in Christian service and ministry, our need is for a constant dependence on the Holy Spirit to be to us what we need and to accomplish through us what only he can do. This does not mean that the Christian does not work hard and apply himself to the use of God-ordained means. But he realizes that in and of himself he is nothing and can do nothing to bear fruit that will glorify God. He must therefore dwell in unceasing dependence on him.

10: *Serving and Loving Others*

Just as in our relationship to God, life in the Spirit is characterized by a desire to give, the same is true in our relationship with others. God is love and those who are born into his family will bear their Father's image: 'Beloved, let us love one another, for love is from God; and everyone who loves is born of God and knows God. The one who does not love does not know God, for God is love' (*1 Jn. 4:7–8*). Love is foundational to everything else in the Christian life. It is the chief fruit of the Spirit. Jonathan Edwards writes:

> The Scriptures represent true religion, as being summarily comprehended in *love*, the chief of the affections, *and the fountain of all others*. So our blessed Saviour represents the matter, in answer to the lawyer who asked him, Which was the great commandment of the law? (*Matt. xxii. 37–40*). 'Jesus said unto him, Thou shalt love the Lord thy God with all thy heart, and with all thy soul, and with all thy mind . . . And the second is like unto it, Thou shalt love thy neighbour as thyself . . .' These two commandments comprehend all the duty prescribed in the law and the prophets. And the apostle Paul makes the same representation of the matter; as in Rom. xiii. 8, 'He that loveth another, hath fulfilled the law.' And verse 10. 'Love is the fulfilling of the law [*cf. Gal. 5:14; 1 Tim. 1:5*] . . . The same apostle speaks of *love*, as the greatest thing in religion, as the essence and soul of it; without which, the greatest knowledge and gifts, the most glaring profession, and every thing else which appertains to religion, are vain and worthless . . . From hence it clearly and certainly appears,

that great part of true religion consists in the affections.
For love is not only one of the affections, *but it is the first and
chief of them, and the fountain of all the others.*[1]

A true Christian, born of the Spirit, will therefore live as
one who is oriented towards serving and loving men, for the
second great commandment, according to Jesus, is: 'You
shall love your neighbor as yourself' (*Mt. 22:39*). But what
does it mean to love others in a biblical sense?

We have already emphasized Christ's words, 'If anyone
wishes to come after Me, let him deny himself, and take up
his cross *daily*, and follow Me' (*Lk. 9:23*). He is emphasizing
that not only the entrance to the kingdom of God, but daily
life in that kingdom, calls the Christian to take up a cross of
self-renunciation. This is fundamental to maintaining a
servant relationship with God and with others, for love is self-
denial for the sake of another: 'We know love by this, that He
laid down His life for us' (*1 Jn. 3:16*). Self-renunciation was
central in the life of Christ and must also be in the life of every
Christian, for it is the heart of a life of love.

We have already seen how Philippians 2:5–11 is foundational for understanding the person of Christ. But Paul also
uses it to summon us to right relationships with our fellow-
men:

Only conduct yourselves in a manner worthy of the gospel
of Christ; so that whether I come and see you or remain
absent, I may hear of you that you are standing firm in one
spirit, with one mind striving together for the faith of the
gospel . . . If therefore there is any encouragement in
Christ, if there is any consolation of love, if there is any
fellowship of the Spirit, if any affection and compassion,
make my joy complete by being of the same mind,
maintaining the same love, united in spirit, intent on one
purpose. Do nothing from selfishness or empty conceit,

[1]*The Works of Jonathan Edwards*, Volume 1, p. 240, (some emphases added).

but with humility of mind let each of you regard one another as more important than himself; do not merely look out for your own personal interests, but also for the interests of others (*Phil. 1:27; 2:1–4*).

Paul's ultimate appeal here is for Christians to conduct their relationships with one another in a manner that is *worthy* of the gospel of Christ. God is glorified when believers live and work together in a spirit of love and unity. But this oneness of spirit and purpose is promoted only when we are committed to humble-mindedness in our relationships with others. Paul appeals to the example of Christ as a basis for this:

Have this attitude in yourselves which was also in Christ Jesus, who, although He existed in the form of God, did not regard equality with God a thing to be grasped, but emptied Himself, taking the form of a bond-servant, and being made in the likeness of men. And being found in appearance as a man, He humbled Himself by becoming obedient to the point of death, even death on a cross (*Phil. 2:5–8*).

Humility of mind is the mindset which Jesus himself possessed in setting aside all concern for self-interest and living for the sake of others. Therefore Paul says, 'Do nothing from selfishness or empty conceit', that is, with a concern to exalt and promote oneself. Here we are exhorted to a life of self-renunciation for the sake of others. Such a life of love will result in unity which in turn will result in the glorifying of God. It becomes a powerful light shining into the darkness of the unregenerate world.

This attitude has a very direct and practical bearing on our relationships with others. We are to consider others as 'more important' than ourselves. We are to be on constant guard against a haughty, superior, condescending attitude towards others. It is true that men differ with respect to their gifts, abilities and talents, since God gifts men and women in different ways. Some, for example, are more capable intellectually, while others may be gifted with artistic or athletic ability or business acumen. Some are given wealth, or social standing and influence. But we must never look upon our capacities and gifts as a cause for self-exaltation for they are gifts from God. John the Baptist said, 'A man can receive nothing, unless it has been given him from heaven' (*Jn. 3:27*). Worldly men may think they are important because of social standing or wealth, education, background, or personal capacities. But that is a delusion, 'for if anyone thinks he is something when he is nothing, he deceives himself' (*Gal. 6:3*).

All too often the world's value system and way of thinking filters into the church. Rather than humility, it is pride that is seen. Sadly, this was so in the Corinthian church, where some members were manifesting haughty and proud attitudes. Spiritual pride (thinking that we are more spiritual or better than others) is deadly to the promotion of love and unity. It brings division. There are numerous ways in which this problem manifests itself. In some instances there is a false view of spiritual gifts. Some think they are superior to others because they possess certain gifts (*cf. 1 Cor. 12*). Or there can be a problem with knowledge: 'Knowledge makes arrogant, but love edifies' (*1 Cor. 8:1*). Where knowledge becomes an end in itself, divorced from a life of practical godliness, it brings pride. Where Christianity is viewed primarily as a system of doctrine, it can easily lead to an attitude of superiority. We begin to adopt a spirit of self-importance because we think that our education or position of spiritual leadership makes us superior. Sadly, leaders in churches may begin to think that the people to whom they are called to minister are there for them rather than the other way round. A congregation can become a means to the promotion of a proud man's personal agenda. He can lose that lowly, servant attitude and use people. Sometimes individuals or groups adopt extra-biblical convictions about external standards of behaviour, such as clothing, hair-styles or food, and they equate spirituality with conformity to their particular rules. This soon breeds spiritual pride and an arrogant, stand-offish attitude towards others who do not conform to those same standards. Then there is the problem of cliques and the promotion and exaltation of spiritual leaders (*cf. 1 Cor. 1*). We may be identified with a particular group or individual and think we are better and more spiritual than others because of our identification with that group or individual. All of these things lead to pride rather than humility. We need to be on our guard constantly against these evidences that we see ourselves as superior to others. Instead we must cultivate a lowly attitude towards ourselves.

If we have a proper and realistic view of our own hearts before God it is impossible to have a superior attitude towards others. Instead we will be able to say with Paul, 'I am the chief of sinners' (*1 Tim. 1:15*), and esteem others above ourselves. John Calvin makes the following comments with respect to this whole issue:

> But it is asked, how it is possible that one who is in reality distinguished above others can reckon those to be superior to him who he knows are greatly beneath him? I answer, that this altogether depends on a right estimate of God's gifts, and our own infirmities. For however any one may be distinguished by illustrious endowments, he ought to consider with himself that they have not been conferred upon him that he might be self-complacent, that he might exalt himself, or even that he might hold himself in esteem. Let him, instead of this, employ himself in correcting and detecting his faults, and he will have abundant occasion for humility. In others, on the other hand, he will regard with honour whatever there is

of excellences, and will by means of love bury their faults. The man who will observe this rule, will feel no difficulty in preferring others before himself.[2]

Within the church, all members are to be of equal status. There should be no class distinctions, no colour barriers. We are all one, each equally beloved of the Lord. That is why we are not to evaluate people as the world evaluates them. The world's acceptance and love is based upon the fulfilment of certain conditions, or upon such criteria as likeability, personality, charisma, appearance, intellect, money, accomplishments, influence, background. This kind of thinking should have no place in the church. We are to have an attitude of mutual acceptance, respect and genuine affection towards one another based solely on the fact that we are all brothers and sisters in Christ. Each one is to be valued for the individual worth he or she possesses in God's eyes. There should be no distinctions, no partiality shown to individuals on the basis of a worldly evaluation:

My brethren, do not hold your faith in our glorious Lord Jesus Christ with an attitude of personal favoritism. For if a man comes into your assembly with a gold ring and dressed in fine clothes, and there also comes in a poor man in dirty clothes, and you pay special attention to the one who is wearing the fine clothes, and say, 'You sit here in a good place,' and you say to the poor man, 'You stand over there, or sit down by my footstool,' have you not made distinctions among yourselves, and become judges with evil motives?

Listen, my beloved brethren: did not God choose the poor of this world to be rich in faith and heirs of the kingdom which He promised to those who love Him? But you have dishonored the poor man. Is it not the rich who

[2]John Calvin, *Calvin's Commentaries*, Volume XXI, *Philippians*, (Grand Rapids: Baker, reprinted 1981), p. 53.

oppress you and personally drag you into court? Do they not blaspheme the fair name by which you have been called? If, however, you are fulfilling the royal law, according to the Scripture, 'You shall love your neighbor as yourself', you are doing well. But if you show partiality, you are committing sin and are convicted by the law as transgressors (*Jas. 2:1–9*).

Though James is dealing specifically with the issue of rich and poor, the overall principle applies to all forms of partiality and distinction whether outwardly or in our minds. They are strictly forbidden. Such attitudes are sinful because they transgress the law of love, and encourage a sinful attitude of pride and self-importance. They wrongly promote the view that some are better than others. No individual in the body of Christ is more important than another, but we *are* to esteem each one as more important than ourselves.

Paul further says that if we are to live out the mind of Christ, we must look out for the personal interests of others and become genuinely concerned for them. Not our own needs, desires or interests, but the needs of others must dominate our lives. The sacrifice of our time, our energies, our material substance and ourselves in prayer and practical service to meet the needs of others, are all involved in true giving. Dr Paul Brand gives a wonderful illustration of what this means in the course of describing his own mother, who spent many years as a missionary in India:

One last figure towers above all others who have influenced my life: my mother, known as Granny Brand. I say it kindly and in love, but in old age my mother had little of physical beauty left in her. She had been a classic beauty as a young woman – I have photographs to prove it – but not in old age. The rugged conditions in India, combined with crippling falls and her battles with typhoid, dysentery, and malaria had made her a thin, hunched-over old woman. Years of exposure to wind and sun had toughened her facial skin into leather and furrowed it with wrinkles as deep and extensive as any I have seen on a human face. She knew better than anyone that her physical appearance had long since failed her – for this reason she adamantly refused to keep a mirror in her house.

At the age of seventy-five, while working in the mountains of South India, my mother fell and broke her hip. She lay all night on the floor in pain until a workman found her the next morning. Four men carried her on a string-and-wood cot down the mountain path to the plains and put her in a jeep for an agonizing 150-mile ride over rutted roads. (She had made this trip before, after a head-first fall off a horse on a rocky mountain path, and already had experienced some paralysis below her knees.)

I soon scheduled a visit to my mother's mud-walled home in the mountains in order to persuade her to retire. By then she could walk only with the aid of two bamboo canes taller than she was, planting the canes and lifting her legs high with each painful step to keep her paralyzed feet from dragging on the ground. Yet she continued to travel on horseback and camp in the outlying villages in order to preach the gospel and treat sicknesses and pull the decayed teeth of the villagers.

I came with compelling arguments for her retirement. It was not safe for her to go on living alone in such a remote place with good help a day's journey away. With her faulty sense of balance and paralyzed legs, she presented a constant medical hazard. Already she had endured fractures of vertebrae and ribs, pressure on her spinal nerve roots, a brain concussion, a fractured femur, and severe infection of her hand. 'Even the best of people do sometimes retire when they reach their seventies,' I said with a smile. 'Why not come to Vellore and live near us?'

Granny threw off my arguments like so much nonsense and shot back a reprimand. Who would continue the work? There was no one else in the entire mountain range to preach, to bind up wounds, and to pull teeth. 'In any case,' she concluded, 'what is the use of preserving my old body if it is not going to be used where God needs me?'

And so she stayed. Eighteen years later, at the age of ninety-three, she reluctantly gave up sitting on her pony because she was falling all too frequently. Devoted Indian villagers began bearing her on a hammock from town to town. After two more years of mission work, she finally died at age ninety-five. She was buried, at her request, in a simple, well-used sheet laid in the ground – no coffin. She abhorred the notion of wasting precious wood on coffins . . .

One of my last and strongest visual memories of my mother is set in a village in the mountains she loved, perhaps the last time I saw her in her own environment. She is sitting on a low stone wall that circles the village, with people pressing in from all sides. They are listening to all she has to say about Jesus. Heads are nodding in encouragement, and deep, searching questions come from the crowd. Granny's own rheumy eyes are shining, and standing beside her I can see what she must be seeing through failing eyes: intent faces gazing with absolute trust and affection on one they have grown to love.[3]

Mrs Brand had every reason to be concerned for herself, but she was not dominated by her own needs and interests. The spiritual and physical interests of other people came first. She had the spirit of her Master, the spirit of sacrifice and self-giving. Our Lord was totally disinterested in himself. His concern was for the spiritual, emotional and physical well-being of others. He put others' needs ahead of his own, at infinite cost to himself.

That same spirit grips the true Christian. Before Hudson Taylor went to China, he had an experience that had a major impact on his life. He used to go to the poor districts of the town in which he was living to share the gospel. One night he was summoned by a distraught father who asked him to come

[3]Paul Brand and Philip Yancey, *In His Image*, (Grand Rapids: Zondervan, 1984), pp. 43–45.

and pray for his family. He followed the man home and walked into a room that was practically devoid of furniture. In the corner was a woman with a baby and several small children; she was obviously very sick. The family had very little clothing or food, no money and no means to pay a doctor. Hudson Taylor had a half-crown in his pocket. It was literally all the money he had in the world, and sufficient to pay for a doctor and buy some food for those people.

He started to pray for them, but he found that he could get nowhere. The words seemed to get stuck in his throat. Then a battle between self-interest and sacrificial love began in his heart. Here before him was incredible need which he could help alleviate, but to do so would leave him penniless. He would have absolutely no money for his own needs. The struggle raged in his heart. Finally, he reached into his pocket and gave everything he had to that family. He later said that at that moment unimaginable joy filled his heart, and he was able to pray. He gave sacrificially, putting the needs and interests of others ahead of his own, and soon God gave back to him all he needed and more. But Hudson Taylor learned a great lesson from that experience: when we leave our case in God's hands, trust him to be our security, giving our all for his sake and the sake of others, he will always provide for us. This was a fact which he proved over and over again in his missionary career.

The law of giving is written into the constitution of the kingdom of God. God himself is always giving for the sake of others. He is constantly giving for this is the essence of grace: 'For you know the grace of our Lord Jesus Christ, that though He was rich, yet for your sake He became poor, that you through His poverty might become rich' (*2 Cor. 8:9*). The Christian life is one of forgetting ourselves and committing our needs to the Lord. In so giving we then receive. This is one of the paradoxes of the kingdom of God, as Scripture indicates:

But seek first His kingdom and His righteousness; and all these things shall be added to you (*Mt. 6:33*).

And if you give yourself to the hungry, and satisfy the desire of the afflicted, then your light will rise in darkness, and your gloom will become like midday. And the Lord will continually guide you, and satisfy your desire in scorched places, and give strength to your bones; and you will be like a watered garden, and like a spring of water whose waters do not fail (*Is. 58:10–11*).

Give to everyone who asks of you, and whoever takes away what is yours, do not demand it back. And just as you want people to treat you, treat them in the same way. And if you love those who love you, what credit is that to you? For even sinners love those who love them. And if you do good to those who do good to you, what credit is that to you? For even sinners do the same. And if you lend to those from whom you expect to receive, what credit is that to you? Even sinners lend to sinners, in order to receive back the same amount. But love your enemies, and do good, and lend, expecting nothing in return; and your reward will be great, and you will be sons of the Most High; for He Himself is kind to ungrateful and evil men. Be merciful, just as your Father is merciful. And do not judge and you will not be judged; and do not condemn, and you will not be condemned; pardon, and you will be pardoned. Give, and it will be given to you; good measure, pressed down, shaken together, running over, they will pour into your lap. For by your standard of measure it will be measured to you in return (*Lk. 6:30–38*).

All of these verses speak of selfless giving of ourselves, our substance, our attitudes and our energies for the Lord and others. He has promised to minister to us and to meet our needs in return. We are not to be self-protective and self-absorbed but selfless, for this is the nature of divine love.

In the upper room, the Lord Jesus washed the disciples' feet (*Jn. 13:1ff.*). The Lord of glory girded a towel about his waist and served his disciples one by one in an act of humble service. He was willing to do the unthinkable: to humble himself and do the lowly task. He did not adopt the attitude that this was beneath him. He took the position of a slave in order to minister. He said, 'I am among you as the one who serves' (*Lk. 22:27*). This incident teaches us a valuable lesson. No task should be thought of as too menial or beneath us. We are to maintain the mindset of the girded towel. And there must be no limit upon our service or to whom we will serve, for Jesus washed Judas' feet also, knowing full well that he would betray him. Jesus served others regardless of their response to him. He served even his enemies.

Paul does not say that we are to look out for the interests of others *if* those interests coincide with our own; or *if* that person loves us and treats us fairly; or *if* it is convenient; or *if* that person is lovable and easy to get along with; or *if* that person appreciates us. We do not serve others because it is convenient, or makes us feel good, or because they are worthy or hopefully they will serve us in return. We serve others *for Jesus' sake*: 'For we do not preach ourselves but Christ Jesus as Lord, and ourselves as your bond-servants for Jesus' sake' (*2 Cor. 4:5*).

It is vital that we remember that it is for Christ's sake that we serve others. There are times when God will allow us to be put in situations where we will be tested. Those whom we serve will not appreciate us or care for us: they may take advantage of us, or simply take us for granted. But if we have committed ourselves to being Christ's servants, we have come to recognize that we do not have any rights; we will serve others for Jesus' sake, regardless of their attitude towards us. It will not be easy, but by God's grace, through the empowering of his Spirit, we will be enabled to do what seems to be impossible.

When Paul first went to Antioch and Iconium to serve people in bringing them the gospel, the Jews incited the multitudes; they stoned him, dragged him outside the city and left him for dead. But God raised him up, and rather than write off the people in disgust, he returned to the very city where he had been stoned. Paul was first and foremost a servant of God. He was enabled to serve these people under such trying circumstances because he was committed to doing the will of God, which was to return and serve them, regardless of the cost to himself. He was willing to put the interests of others ahead of his own. The cross stood at the very centre of his servant life. We must take it up daily in order to deny ourselves and die to self-interest. Only then can we give ourselves in a sacrificial way to others.

Serving others does not mean regarding them as more important than ourselves and putting their interests ahead of our own in a mechanical sort of way. I remember a missionary from Thailand telling the following story about a wealthy Buddhist and a beggar. The missionary happened to be looking through his window one morning when he saw a beggar approach the front door of a wealthy man's home begging for food. The man seemed to take pity on the beggar and gave him a great deal of food. Naturally the missionary was impressed with what he had witnessed and at his first opportunity he made a comment to his neighbour about the generosity and love he had shown. But the Buddhist corrected him. He said, quite emphatically, that he did not love the man at all, but in fact despised him as filthy and worthless. The only reason that he gave to him, he said, was that it would help his *karma* – he regarded his action as a good deed that would help him in the afterlife. He had rendered a service which, from all outward appearance, seemed to be full of love; yet it was totally selfish in motive. There was no concern, no genuine affection for the individual. He was actually intending to promote his own interests. He was using the man and, even though he was serving him in a technical sense, he did not love him.

Paul further amplifies the teaching of Philippians 2:1–11 in his letter to the Ephesians:

> I, therefore, the prisoner of the Lord, entreat you to walk in a manner worthy of the calling with which you have been called, with all humility and gentleness, with patience, showing forbearance to one another in love, being diligent to preserve the unity of the Spirit in the bond of peace (*Eph. 4:1–3*).

Again, Paul is emphasizing the importance of walking in a way that is worthy of our calling and of preserving and promoting unity. Unity does not just *happen*. It must be diligently and zealously pursued and maintained. Because of the strategic importance of this unity in bringing glory to God and in overcoming the kingdom of darkness, the devil makes every effort to destroy it. That is why we have to fight to maintain it by spiritual watchfulness, and by maintaining certain attitudes in our relationships with one another. Paul tells us specifically what those attitudes are: the walk which is worthy of our calling is characterized by humility, meekness, patience, and forbearance or longsuffering.

Note that Paul begins with humility and meekness. Without them it is impossible to live in an attitude of patience and forbearance towards others. Humility and meekness primarily have to do with our relationship with God, while patience and forbearance have to do with our relationship with men. What does this mean in practice?

We have seen in some detail that humility involves realizing our own helplessness, and turning from all self-reliance, self-exaltation and self-promotion to live in dependence upon God. It means taking a lowly view of ourselves, casting ourselves in dependence upon the Lord for his enabling to fulfil his calling.

The second major characteristic Paul mentions is meekness. The Greek word is *praotes* which generally means 'gentleness' or 'mildness'. But those definitions do not adequately describe the exact meaning of the word. A. W. Pink brings out its significance as follows:

> And now we have meekness as a by-product of self-emptying and self-humiliation; or, in other words, there is a broken will and a receptive heart before God. Meekness is not only the antithesis of pride, but of stubbornness, fierceness, vengefulness. It is the taming of the lion, the making of the wolf to lie down as a kid . . . 'The meekness to which the blessing is annexed is not constitutional, but *gracious*: and men of the most vehement, impetuous, irascible, and implacable dispositions, by looking to Jesus through the grace of God, learn to curb their tempers, to cease from resentment, to avoid giving offence by injurious words and actions, to make concessions and forgive injuries.'
>
> Meekness is the opposite of *self-will* toward God, and of *ill-will* toward men. 'The meek are those who quietly submit themselves before God, to His Word, to His rod, who follow His directions and comply with His designs, and are gentle toward men' (Matthew Henry) . . . Inasmuch as meekness is that spirit which has been schooled to mildness by discipline and suffering, and brought into sweet resignation to the will of God, it causes the believer to bear patiently those insults and injuries which he receives at the hands of his fellows, and makes him ready to accept instruction or admonition from the least of the saints, moving him to think more highly of others than of himself. Meekness enables the Christian to endure provocations without being inflamed by them: he remains cool when others get heated.[4]

Meekness, as Pink shows, has both a Godward and a manward aspect. The meek are those who have committed themselves unreservedly to the will of God and to whatever

[4]A. W. Pink, *An Exposition of the Sermon on the Mount*, Swengel, Pa. (reprinted by Baker Book House, Grand Rapids) pp. 22–23.

he allows into their lives in the way of both people and circumstances. True meekness responds to both people and circumstances in a way that is consistent with the will of God. In relationships with others, meekness has to do with one's reaction to trials. The perfect example of this is the Lord Jesus himself: 'And while being reviled, He did not revile in return; while suffering He uttered no threats, but kept entrusting Himself to Him who judges righteously' (*1 Pet. 2:23*). Jesus did not return evil for evil, or insult for insult. He submitted to the will of God and responded in love, even in the midst of his trial. He was meek. This is the attitude which is the foundation for a life of love towards others, and in fulfilling Paul's exhortations for patience and forbearance. Only the humble and meek can live in patience and forbearance towards others, and thus preserve the unity of the Spirit in the bond of peace.

The Greek verb for being patient is *makrothumeō*. According to *Thayer's Greek-English Lexicon of the New Testament*, it means 'to be of a long spirit, not to lose heart; to be patient in bearing the offences and injuries of others; to be mild and slow in avenging; to be long-suffering, slow to anger, slow to punish'. Patience is the outworking of an attitude of meekness towards others. It is restraint in the face of provocation. In looking at this whole issue in chapter nine we dealt mainly with the individual's attitude towards God in accepting any and all circumstances from his hand. But the meek person is also concerned to react to people in a righteous way for this is also part of doing the will of God. Thus patience means more than simply accepting a trial from someone, and enduring it. For the word also encompasses one's attitude towards the person who is the source of the trial.

It is all too possible to be outwardly gentle and submissive under trial and yet inwardly resentful, unforgiving and bitter in our hearts. That results in coldness and a withdrawing of affection from the individual. In 1 Corinthians 13:4 the word 'patience' is followed immediately by the word 'kindness'. In Christian love, patience and kindness belong together. We can endure trial from another person but withhold our hearts from them and refuse to love and serve them in an active sense. But not only must we endure, we must continue to serve and to be kind, not taking into account a wrong suffered. We must be willing to forgive, to forget ourselves and to continue to love. This takes a firm commitment of the will and a constant looking to the Lord to help us to love as he loves. We must resolutely refuse bitterness, anger, resentment, and an unforgiving, critical spirit. This involves dying to ourselves and our supposed rights and living as servants of God who are committed to living in love with others. Another person may malign us, lie about us, betray us or mistreat us. We must resist the temptation to cut that person off in our hearts and withdraw from them. By the grace of God we are to love them, serve them and pray for them.

If we allow ourselves to become bitter and resentful because of what someone has done to us, we have abandoned the servant spirit. We are not willingly accepting the circumstances of God's choosing and positively doing the will of God in those circumstances in our attitude towards the one who has wronged us. We have allowed ourselves to become self-oriented, and have turned from the way of the cross and obedience to the will of God. An unforgiving spirit, bitterness, resentment, anger and self-pity are contrary to the will of God. Love, if it is true biblical love, can still operate in the atmosphere in which there is much that is unfair, unjust, unloving, unkind and difficult. It is not a hard thing to love and serve someone who loves us and serves us in return. But Christ-like love goes beyond the merely natural and does that which, by the grace of God, is supernatural. It washes the feet of a Judas. It prays for its enemies. It serves those who malign and despise it. It does not protect self and withdraw. It forgets self and accepts the unacceptable. And

in a positive active sense it loves and serves for Jesus' sake
and for the sake of others.

Living such a life is obviously not easy or free from pain.
There is a personal cost involved in it, for it means a death to
natural feelings. It means a willingness to absorb emotional
or physical pain caused by others without reacting in kind.

In the Christian life we always need to fix our eyes on the
Lord Jesus Christ. Much that happened to him was unfair. It
was neither right nor just. But he served in the midst of it. He
accepted the circumstances of God's choosing and he did not
allow those circumstances to turn him against people, not
even when he was on the cross. This same disposition is given
to those who are his servants. It is not just an ideal to be
admired, but a life-style actually to be lived. And it is lived
by those who truly know Jesus Christ.

The final phrase that Paul uses in Ephesians 4:2 is
'forbearing one another in love'. The word 'to forbear' is the
Greek word *anexō*, which means 'to hold up, to hold one's
self erect and firm, to sustain, to bear, to bear with, endure'
(*Thayer's Greek-English Lexicon of the New Testament*). The
general meaning of the word is very similar to what is
involved in patience. It carries the basic idea of making
allowances for one another's frailties and mistakes, of
'overlooking and forgiving many things in the conduct of our
brethren', as John Calvin puts it. We realize we are not
perfect, we have many personal failings and shortcomings
and we are going to deal with others as we would want them
to deal with us. We are to make allowances for the frailties
and human condition of others. We do not get out our list
and demand that individuals conform to our expectations.
We accept people where they are, love them uncondition-
ally and with genuine affection and compassion and especially during a time of failure. There is to be a forbearing or
longsuffering spirit with love. This re-emphasizes what we
noted before about patience and kindness. It is not simply a

matter of enduring, but of having a loving attitude towards the brother or sister in the midst of the difficulty. We need to learn not to focus on people's shortcomings, failures and personality quirks, but instead to commit ourselves in a positive way to love them, accept them and express genuine affection for them.

Christian love, therefore, is not just the absence of negative attitudes such as bitterness, anger and resentment. It is also positive. It reaches out to people. God's love not only forgives us; it also accepts us and brings us into a relationship of genuine affection. We are to live in that same love.

The apostle Paul exemplified this love in his relationships. 'God is my witness,' he said, 'how I long for you all with the affection of Christ Jesus' (*Phil. 1:8*). Again he says, 'Having thus a fond affection for you, we were well-pleased to impart to you not only the gospel of God but also our own lives, because you had become very dear to us' (*1 Thess. 2:8*). He speaks in very tender terms about the real affection he had for them, and says specifically that it came from the Lord Jesus Christ. There is no hint here of a stand-offish or cool spirit towards others. We should all be very careful never to be responsible for causing anyone to feel rejected. This is part of what it means to be a servant of God who walks not only in forbearance but in love. As William Hendriksen puts it: 'Paul . . . very aptly combines the forbearance of which he is speaking with the inner disposition of love. He everywhere emphasizes this virtue of outgoingness, true and tender affection toward the brother, the neighbor, and even the enemy, the noble endeavor to benefit him and never to harm him in any way.'[5]

We need to commit ourselves to seeing the potential in men and women for change through the grace of God, rather than concentrating critically upon their negative features. This is not to say that we put our heads in the sand and refuse

[5]William Hendriksen, *Ephesians*, in *Galatians and Ephesians*, (Grand Rapids: Baker, 1967), p. 184.

to be honest about others' faults. But it does mean that we are committed to making allowances for their frailties and mistakes, and that we do not allow our affection for them to be quenched. We must never write off an individual in our hearts, for whatever reason. We will be less likely to do so if we commit ourselves to praying for them.

This is not to say that in doing this all our relationships will be open and free of misunderstanding. At times others may raise barriers in the relationship which hinder openness of communication. This is why Paul says, 'If possible, so far as it depends on you, be at peace with all men' (*Rom. 12:18*). My responsibility is to make sure that I am doing all that God would have *me* do in order to maintain unity with others. For by the grace of God we are committed to considering others as more important than ourselves, to giving ourselves in sacrificial ways and putting others' interests ahead of our own.

OPPOSITION AND CONFLICT

There is a balancing truth to what we have been saying, and it too should be emphasized. As Christians we must never forget that we are first and foremost servants of God. The commitment to serve men must never be allowed to displace our primary commitment to God. While we are called to be servants *to* men, we are never to be enslaved by them. The will of God alone is to be the final authority in our lives.

To be Christ's disciples means that we will experience the reality of opposition and conflict:

Do not think that I came to bring peace on the earth; I did not come to bring peace, but a sword. For I came to set a man against his father, and a daughter against her mother, and a daughter-in-law against her mother-in-law; and a man's enemies will be the members of his household. He who loves father or mother more than Me is not worthy of Me (*Mt. 10:34–37*).

As Christians, we are taught that there is a conflict which may affect the closest relationships and extend out into the society in which we live. Conflict cannot be avoided if we would be true to our Lord and live for his will as a matter of priority. It is the inevitable result of giving exclusive allegiance to Jesus Christ in being his servant. His values become our values, his longings our longings, his objectives our objectives, his desires our desires, his will our will, and his cause our cause. And all of this brings us into direct opposition with those who are opposed to the Lord Jesus Christ and his gospel.

But in the face of such conflict, God repeatedly instructs us: 'Do not fear, for I am with you' (*Is. 41:10*). Fear is not of God. 'For God has not given us a spirit of timidity, but of power and love and discipline' (*2 Tim. 1:7*). We are not to live in the fear of man any more than we live for the approval and acceptance of others. As servants of God we are not to allow the fear of being rejected and ostracized, of being maligned or considered odd to control us, for then we would be the servants of men rather than the servants of God.

Paul has some very sober words to say regarding this whole issue:

As we have said before, so I say again now, if any man is preaching to you a gospel contrary to that which you received, let him be accursed. For am I now seeking the favor of men, or of God? Or am I striving to please men? If I were still trying to please men, I would not be a bond-servant of Christ (*Gal. 1:9–10*).

Paul could have avoided conflict simply by refusing to take a stand for the truth. If he had been seeking to please men or been concerned to avoid personal inconvenience, that is what he would have done. But Paul's primary concern was not the acceptance of men but the approval of God. He was God's servant, not man's. So he was willing to face conflict for the sake of his master. He was not looking for peace and unity at any cost.

We have already seen that Paul was deeply concerned about unity – but unity that is grounded on the truth of God's Word. There can be no true biblical unity at the expense of truth, especially the essential truths of the gospel. I recently had a discussion with a pastor who confided that he thought the controversy surrounding 'Lordship salvation' (which we discussed earlier) was divisive. I agreed with him. Truth *is* divisive when it comes against falsehood. But that kind of division and conflict is not wrong. As servants of Christ we must be willing to die to our natural desires to be accepted. We have no option; we *must* stand for the truth of the gospel. We must love those who oppose the truth, but that does not mean that we acquiesce to them. If we give in to the fear of being rejected by men and seek peace at any cost, then we will have turned aside from being the servants of Jesus Christ. We cannot live for men in this way and, at the same time, live for Christ.

This principle is seen in the lives of many of the rulers in Israel during Christ's ministry: 'Nevertheless many even of the rulers believed in Him, but because of the Pharisees they were not confessing Him, lest they should be put out of the synagogue; for they loved the approval of men rather than the approval of God' (*Jn. 12:42–43*). The fear of man prevented them from becoming God's servants and from doing the will of God. But the true servant has died to the world and the approval of men; he lives to show himself approved to God alone. He realizes he is in a conflict, but he also knows that his Lord has promised the necessary grace to be able to stand in the midst of the pressure. This is the lesson we learn from the Hebrew youths in the Book of Daniel. They refused to bow down to the king's image, even though it could mean death. They refused to be turned aside from the will of God by the threats of men. They were servants of God and although this brought them into conflict they stood firm and did not try to avoid it. The glory of God was uppermost in their minds. Note the answer they gave to the king when he threatened to throw them into the furnace:

> If it be so, our God whom we serve is able to deliver us from the furnace of blazing fire; and He will deliver us out of your hand, O king. But even if He does not, let it be known to you, O king, that we are not going to serve your gods or worship the golden image that you have set up (*Dan. 3:17–18*).

A. W. Pink makes these comments about such meekness:

> Meekness must not be confounded with weakness. True meekness is ever manifested by yieldedness to God's will, yet it will not yield a principle of righteousness or compromise with evil. God-given meekness can also stand up for God-given rights: when God's glory is impeached, we must have a zeal which is as hot as fire. Moses was 'very meek, above all the men which were upon the face of the earth' (Num. xii, 3), yet when he saw the Israelites dancing before the golden calf, in zeal for Jehovah's honour, he broke the two tables of stone, and put to the sword those who had transgressed. Note how firmly and boldly the apostles stood their ground in Acts xvi, 35–37. Above all, remember how Christ Himself, in concern for His Father's glory, made a whip of cords and drove the desecrators out of the temple. Meekness restrains from private revenge, but it in nowise conflicts with the requirements of fidelity to God, His cause, and His people.[6]

We have seen that meekness is essential if we would promote love and unity. It is characterized by an absence of

---

[6]A. W. Pink, *An Exposition of the Sermon on the Mount*, p. 24.

self-will towards others. However, the meek man is not one who has no real strength of character – a weak man who simply goes along with the crowd, never rocking the boat. Rather, the meek man is first and foremost committed to the will of God and to promoting his cause. He refuses any cowardly shrinking from conflict. He does not ignore the need to deal with sin when the situation demands it. He will not allow the fear of man to cause him to compromise his relationship with God.

As servants of God we cannot have an indifferent attitude towards sin in those who claim to be our brothers and sisters in Christ. Scripture tells us that those who are spiritual are humbly and gently to confront a brother or sister who is living in open sin (*Gal. 6:1; Mt. 18:15–17*). This is not a pleasant thing to have to do. If we are living for the approval and favour of men we will never do it. But for our Lord's sake and out of obedience to him as his servants we must not shrink from this responsibility, for his glory is at stake. Out of true love, we must confront those who have sinned, in the hope that they may be restored in their relationship with God. To refuse to do this is ultimately to love ourselves more than our Lord or others, for we are simply seeking to protect ourselves from conflict.

As servants of God we are called to serve men. But we must always keep before us the truth that we are servants *of* God and servants *to* men. Where man's will brings us into conflict with God's will we must put God first, no matter what the cost to ourselves.

Conclusion

Throughout these pages we have seen that the pre-eminent example of true Christianity is the life of Christ. He is the ultimate pattern of what life in the Spirit really means. And when the Holy Spirit brings an individual into the experience of the new birth, his new life will begin to conform to the character and life of the Lord Jesus, portrayed in the Word of God. The Christian life is not merely an imitation of the life of Jesus but it is the manifestation of his very life. Nothing less is true of all those who have been brought into union with Christ and indwelt by the Spirit of God. Whatever was characteristic of the life of Jesus becomes characteristic of all who live in the Spirit. The same principles which governed and dominated the life of Christ will be evidenced in the life of every true believer: the glory of God, the servant heart, faith, communion, prayer, obedience, love and the kingdom of God.

These principles and their relationship to one another are illustrated in the diagram on the following page. From the diagram we see that the over-arching principle, which represents the great objective of the Christian life, is the glory of God. He is glorified through the individual's living out these other principles. But note that foundational to all that is listed along the horizontal line is the servant heart. Apart from that foundation none of the other things will be a reality in anyone's life because, without it, there is no true conversion.

We can summarize the central burden of this book by two final references to Scripture: 'By this is My Father glorified,

The Glory of God

Faith   Communion   Prayer
(Worship)
(Intercession)   Obedience
(Holiness)   Love   Great
Commission
(Ministry)

The Holy Spirit

Servant Heart
(Submission/Humility/Meekness)

that you bear much fruit, and so prove to be My disciples'
(*Jn. 15:8*). Jesus is saying that God is glorified by fruit. So the
ultimate objective of glorifying God is achieved *through* the
bearing of fruit. This proves that one is a Christian or
disciple. What is fruit? That is explained in Romans 6:22,
which we have already examined in some detail, 'But now
having been freed from sin and enslaved to God, you derive
your benefit [fruit], resulting in sanctification, and the
outcome, eternal life.' Fruit is a sanctified life. According to
John 15:8, therefore, it is a sanctified life that glorifies God.
And what is the foundation for a life of fruit in sanctification?
Romans 6:22 says it is being set free from sin and *enslaved* to
God. It is becoming a servant of God. The foundation to a life
of glorifying God, therefore, is a servant heart. Only a
servant of God can truly live a life of prayer in worship,
communion and intercession; only a servant can live by faith,
walk in the Spirit, live a life of holiness and love, fulfil the
great commission and thereby glorify God.

All too often these major principles are taught and
emphasized apart from the foundation of true conversion and
the servant heart. The result has been a dead Christianity.

Today we have much in the way of activities, programmes
and knowledge of theology and principles, but very little in
the way of reality and power and life. The Christian life is not
a matter of simply making a profession, or of having a
knowledge of the Word of God, or of being involved in
ministry. It is a *life* that is to be lived – the life of the Spirit – a
life oriented towards the will of God for his glory. But much
present-day evangelicalism has drifted from the plain
teaching of Scripture on the nature of true conversion and the
Christian life. In many ways the Christian life has been
presented as something self-centred and self-exalting; we
are paying a terrible price both within and without the
church for the abandonment of the biblical gospel and the
truth of Scripture on this subject. We have settled for the
shell of knowledge and ministry to the exclusion of the
genuine life of the indwelling Spirit.

Although J. C. Ryle lived and wrote in the nineteenth
century, his words have as much application to us today as
they did in his generation. They challenge us to face the Word
of God soberly and to return to biblical Christianity:

It may be that a certain profession of religion has become
so fashionable and comparatively easy in the present age,
that the streams which were once narrow and deep have
become wide and shallow, and what we have gained in
outward show we have lost in quality. It may be that the
vast increase in wealth in the last twenty-five years has
insensibly introduced a plague of worldliness, and self-
indulgence, and love of ease into social life. What were
once called luxuries are now comforts and necessaries, and
self-denial and 'enduring hardness' are consequently little
known. It may be that the enormous amount of controversy which marks this age has insensibly dried up our
spiritual life. We have too often been content with zeal for
orthodoxy, and have neglected the sober realities of daily
practical godliness . . . We must return to first principles.
We must go back to 'the old paths.' We must sit down

[158]

humbly in the presence of God, look the whole subject in the face, examine clearly what the Lord Jesus calls sin, and what the Lord Jesus calls 'doing His will.' We must then try to realize that it is *terribly possible* to live a careless, easy-going, half-worldly life, and yet at the same time to maintain Evangelical principles and call ourselves Evangelical people . . .

But to walk closely with God – to be really spiritually-minded – to behave like strangers and pilgrims – to be distinct from the world in employment of time, in conversation, in amusements, in dress – to bear a faithful witness for Christ in all places – to leave a savour of our Master in every society – to be prayerful, humble, unselfish, good-tempered, quiet, easily pleased, charitable, patient, meek – to be jealously afraid of all manner of sin, and tremblingly alive to our danger from the world – these, these are still rare things! They are not common among those who are called true Christians, and, worst of all, the absence of them is not felt and bewailed as it should be.[1]

[1] J. C. Ryle, *Holiness*, pp. 13–14, 161–162.